WITHDRAWN

MA RAINEY'S BLACK BOTTOM

1927

MA RAINEY'S BLACK BOTTOM

1927

AUGUST WILSON

FOREWORD BY FRANK RICH

THEATRE COMMUNICATIONS GROUP
NEW YORK
2007

The August Wilson Century Cycle is funded in part by the Ford Foundation, with additional support from The Paul G. Allen Family Foundation, The Heinz Endowments and the New York State Council on the Arts.

TCG books are exclusively distributed to the book trade by Consortium Book Sales and Distribution, 1045 Westgate Drive, St. Paul, MN 55114.

LIBRARY OF CONGRESS CATALOGING-IN-PUBLICATION DATA
Wilson, August.
Ma Rainey's black bottom / August Wilson ; foreword by Frank Rich.—1st ed.
    p. cm.—(August Wilson century cycle)
        ISBN-13: 978-1-55936-299-3 (vol.)
        ISBN-10: 1-55936-299-5 (vol.)
        ISBN-13: 978-1-55936-307-5 (set)
        ISBN-10: 1-55936-307-X (set)
    1. Rainey, Ma 1886-1939—Drama. 2. Blues musicians—Drama.
3. Nineteen twenties—Drama. 4. Chicago (Ill.)—Drama. I. Title.
        PS3573.I45677M3   2007
        812'.54—dc22   2007022087

Text design and composition by Lisa Govan
Slipcase and cover design by John Gall
Cover photograph from the Frank Diggs Collection/Getty Images
Slipcase photographs by Dana Lixenberg (author) and David Cooper

First Edition, September 2007

For my mother

FOREWORD

by Frank Rich

EARLY IN MY CAREER as the *New York Times* chief drama critic, I made my first pilgrimage to The O'Neill Theater Center in Waterford, Connecticut. The O'Neill's National Playwrights Conference was conceived by its founder, George C. White, as a sort of summer camp for new American dramatists. The competition to get into the Conference was arduous—August Wilson's first submitted play, *Jitney*, had been rejected twice before *Ma Rainey's Black Bottom* gained him entry in 1982, the year of my visit. The reward for those like Wilson who made the grade was to watch Equity actors and professional directors bring their plays to life in staged readings performed within a bustling complex of makeshift stages and dorms strewn over a gorgeous piece of real estate on Long Island Sound. Critics were allowed to visit The O'Neill (some critics were on staff as literary advisers to the playwrights), but the deal was that they didn't "review" what they saw. The point of The O'Neill was to shield green writers and their embryonic works from the pressures of the commercial theater—producers, agents and the press.

With good reason. It was the commercial theater, after all, that had imprisoned and embittered James O'Neill, the turn-of-the-century matinee idol who was memorialized in his son's masterpiece *Long Day's Journey into Night*. (The O'Neill family summer home, where that nominally disguised autobiographical play was set, is in New London, a short drive from The O'Neill complex.) Eugene O'Neill, too, had railed against the commercial theater and been tragically victimized by it. *A Moon for the Misbegotten* had closed in its pre-Broadway tryout after poor reviews and censorship problems; it would not get a first-class New York production until decades after his death. Another late O'Neill masterpiece, *The Iceman Cometh*, was a Broadway flop; its length and downbeat vision didn't mesh with the postwar commercial theater, and it too would have to be rescued (Off-Broadway, by the young theatrical newcomers José Quintero and Jason Robards, Jr.) when its author was no longer around to see it.

This history was very much in my mind as I watched the first performance of *Ma Rainey* in one of The O'Neill's outdoor spaces on a typically hot and humid summer night. Even by the standards of The O'Neill, where the plays were still so new they had yet to be subjected to serious editing, *Ma Rainey* was long—nearly *Iceman Cometh* length. As always at these readings, there were no sets or costumes. Though the characters were musicians, there were no musical instruments: any "playing" was mimed by the actors. Given the heat, the running time and the insects, not all the audience stayed till the end. Those who left early would later learn they missed what remains one of the shocking denouements of American drama, an act of self-immolation that seems to echo through the entire tortured history of race in America.

Another chapter of theater history was on my mind as well that July night. I was keenly aware that the director of *Ma Rainey* was Lloyd Richards, the Yale Drama School dean who had been recruited by George White to be The O'Neill's artistic director at the conference's inception eighteen years earlier. Richards loomed large in my own theater-going history. As a stage-struck child growing up in Washington, D.C., I had had few more formative experiences than seeing the original Broadway production of Lorraine Hansberry's *A Raisin in the Sun* in its post-Broadway tour. (Claudia McNeil and Diana Sands were still in the cast; Sidney Poitier by then had decamped for Hollywood.) Richards, in a professional first for an African American in the Broadway theater, was the play's director. Back then—I was twelve—I didn't know exactly what a director did, but I did know that *Raisin*, written by a black woman and directed by a black man, was already a legendary breakthrough.

And I certainly was beginning to learn what racism was. Growing up in 1950s Washington—in the city itself, not the suburbs—it was hard to ignore the reality that the nation's capital was more or less as run as a plantation. Though the city was technically "desegregated," de facto segregation was a given, with the city's neighborhoods, business establishments and public facilities (including schools) all unofficially and rigidly divvied up by race. As if to mock the idealistic democratic sentiments enshrined in the city's alabaster federal buildings visited by tourists and schoolchildren, the city was governed by an entirely white committee of racist Southern congressmen (in those days, Democrats) who regarded the town as their personal fiefdom. Washington's citizens had no vote, not even in presidential elections.

Arriving in this Washington in 1961, as the modern civil rights movement was just beginning to pick up steam, *A Raisin in the Sun* was explosive. The theater where it was booked, the National, was the city's only stop for Broadway tours in those pre–Kennedy Center days, and the house had its own charged racial history. Its owners had notoriously refused to desegregate after segregation was outlawed by the courts, and Equity had responded by refusing to allow its members to perform there. For some years the National tried to duck the issue by operating as a movie theater while Broadway plays stopped instead at an old burlesque house a few blocks away in old downtown D.C. But by the time *Raisin* arrived, new owners had reopened the National as a legitimate playhouse, and, technically at least, all audiences were welcome. (Few blacks went there even so, understandably enough.) To see Hansberry's drama at the National at that juncture in its and Washington's history was a particularly freighted experience. Its portrait of a black family being thwarted by white America filled in a lot of the blanks in my early education about America and race. The Younger family's travails made manifest what was going on all around me in Washington but that few white people in my experience ever talked about explicitly, at least in front of kids. *A Raisin in the Sun* was also the first time I encountered any kind of drama in which black characters of various stripes and generations spoke candidly among themselves, without white characters serving as foils or intermediaries. This was not an experience yet on tap in either Hollywood movies or on network television.

Though *Ma Rainey* shared Lloyd Richards as its artistic godfather and Chicago as its setting, Wilson's play marches to a different beat from Hansberry's. It is set in 1927, three decades earlier than *Raisin*, and it inevitably reflects the sensibility of its author's own generation and circumstances, as well as his calling as a poet. Yet in this early work, the Hansberry-Wilson theatrical lineage is transparent. Wilson shares with his illustrious forebear an affection for lyrical theatrical naturalism, a commitment to conveying the African as well as the American component of the African American experience and, most of all, an insistence that black characters be their full selves on stage rather than domesticated symbols enacting a pro forma liberal civics lesson for the delectation of white audiences.

But in *Ma Rainey*, the characters have no aspirations to make their way into the suburban middle class. The title character, the blues singer Gertrude (Ma) Rainey (1886–1939), is a larger-than-life "success" story. Blues music ("life's way of talking," as one Wilson line has it) had begun to cross over to white audiences, and, along with Bessie Smith, Rainey was among the first black singers to secure a recording contract with a white label, Paramount (or at least its "race" division).

Ma Rainey is set in its entirety in a recording studio, where Rainey is laying down tracks with a small band. This singer could hardly be further removed in personality and circumstances from the humble domestic matriarch of *Raisin*. As a star, she's used to getting her own way, by dint of her talent and by the force of her personality. Her rewards include the timeless accoutrements of American show business glory: an expensive car, an entourage of flunkies, a young and kept (lesbian) plaything. Like other divas, regardless of race or era, she barks out demands to test the limits of her power. The most outrageous is her insistence that her nephew, a chronic stutterer, record a spoken introduction to her songs.

Still, for all her grandiose airs and ego, Rainey retains a core of ferocious realism. "As soon as they get my voice down on them recording machines," she says, "then it's just like if I'd be some whore and they roll over and put their pants on." She knows that the minute she leaves the domain of the recording studio, she will not be able to hail a cab on the streets of Chicago.

Regal and glittery as Rainey is, she has not completely severed her connection to the tender origins of her music. "You don't sing to feel better," she explains. "You sing 'cause that's a way of understanding life." Wilson constructs the play as if it too were music, set forth to understand life. The studio musicians have their own riffs on the play's themes, long soliloquies, by turns rending and funny, that in their seeming spontaneity and kaleidoscopic variations become the verbal and theatrical equivalent of a jam session. Along the way the various solos sketch a history of the black Diaspora stretching from Africa to the American back roads of the musicians' itinerant careers, their horrific encounters with racist violence included.

Of these sidemen, one is more equal than the others: Levee, a young hot-headed trumpeter who is impatient to get his own slice of success and see his name in lights. He has challenged Ma Rainey by writing his own swinging arrangement of the song "Ma Rainey's Black Bottom." He views his version as a jazzy modern antidote to the singer's outmoded "jug-band music" and more in keeping with the new musical fashions sweeping the dance floors of the urban North. Not unlike another mythic young show business climber of roughly that same American era—Sammy Glick in Budd Schulberg's novel *What Makes Sammy Run?*—Levee literally starts his climb up the ladder of success by investing hard-won dollars in a slick pair of shoes. But the obstacles in his path are far greater than those the Jewish Sammy faces in 1930s Hollywood.

Some of Levee's obstacles are from within. "We done sold ourselves to the white man in order to be like him," observes one of his colleagues, the pianist, Toledo. In *Ma Rainey*, it is impossible for all the characters, but most of all Levee, to throw off a legacy of racism that is far more subtle than the brutal facts of discrimination alone—a self-hatred that comes from buying into the white man's values. As Toledo suggests, both Ma and Levee are in some ways "imitation white men" who have compromised their own identities "to become someone else." In this context, Ma Rainey's insistence on clinging to her own music, her refusal to pander to changing popular taste by adopting Levee's arrangement of her song, seems like a valiant stand against a majority culture that is far more powerful than her own. A valiant stand, but perhaps a last stand as well.

For all the play's digressional interludes and seeming plotlessness, its conflicts steadily build to a hugely theatrical climax. It was hard to watch *Ma Rainey* in its first airing at The O'Neill without thinking of *Iceman Cometh* (and not just because of its length). The plays are both marked by claustrophobia, a slow-fuse dramatic structure, meaty arias, a devastating dramatic payoff and their authors' profound identification with those who are betrayed by the gaudy promise of the American dream.

It was also impossible for this young drama critic to resist the siren call of journalism—the desire to get news out fast—and so I ended up half-violating The O'Neill's rule about press coverage: I wrote a column for the *Times* in which I talked in general terms about the excitement generated by a new and unknown playwright's voice on that July Connecticut night.

As it would turn out, the commercial system of the American theater, which had done so much damage to serious playwrights like Eugene O'Neill, would not do the same to August Wilson. Lloyd Richards and a colleague at Yale, the producer Ben Mordecai, would gradually develop a more protected producing paradigm to present *Ma Rainey* and subsequent Wilson plays to the commercial mass audience. Each play would have its premiere in the not-for-profit confines of the Yale Repertory Theatre, where Richards was artistic director, and then take a circuitous route to Broadway via other not-for-profit resident theaters, from Boston to Seattle to Los Angeles. This attenuated process would allow Wilson to steadily revise his work before it faced the ruthless economics of Broadway and the often capricious taste of its ticket buyers. Not all his plays would prove commercially successful on Broadway, but all would have an extended life beyond the original New York run. Most of the original productions would also introduce audiences to new or neglected actors whose careers would take off after appearing in a powerhouse Wilson role, starting with Charles S. Dutton, the original Levee, in *Ma Rainey*.

"Where the hell was God when all of this was going on?" Levee asks as he confronts his demons during the play's corrosive climax. That rhetorical question would be addressed again and again by Wilson as he pursued his epic cycle of plays tackling the African American experience decade by decade. *Ma Rainey*, the first of these plays to be produced in New York and the only one of them not set in Wilson's birthplace, the Hill District of Pittsburgh, would open at the Cort Theatre on Broadway two years after its premiere at The O'Neill and a quarter century after Lorraine Hansberry and Lloyd Richards's Broadway breakthrough with *A Raisin in the Sun*. It would run the better part of the 1984–85 season and receive a major Broadway revival in 2003. All in all, Wilson would live to see eight of the plays in his cycle produced on Broadway during his lifetime, the fruits of a remarkable two-decade burst of creativity that has few parallels in the history of the American theater and that only his premature death could bring to a close.

Frank Rich is an op-ed columnist at the New York Times, *where he served as chief drama critic from 1980–1993.*

MA RAINEY'S BLACK BOTTOM

1927

Production History

Ma Rainey's Black Bottom was initially presented as a staged reading at The Eugene O'Neill Theater Center's 1982 National Playwrights Conference.

Ma Rainey's Black Bottom opened on April 6, 1984, at the Yale Repertory Theatre in New Haven, Connecticut. It was directed by Lloyd Richards; the set design was by Charles Henry McClennahan, the costume design was by Daphne Pascucci, the lighting design was by Peter Maradudin; the music director was Dwight Andrews. The cast was as follows:

STURDYVANT	Richard M. Davidson
IRVIN	Lou Criscuolo
CUTLER	Joe Seneca
TOLEDO	Robert Judd
SLOW DRAG	Leonard Jackson
LEVEE	Charles S. Dutton
MA RAINEY	Theresa Merritt
POLICEMAN	David Wayne Nelson
DUSSIE MAE	Sharon Mitchell
SYLVESTER	Steven R. Blye

Ma Rainey's Black Bottom opened on October 11, 1984, at the Cort Theatre on Broadway in New York City. It was directed by Lloyd Richards; the set design was by Charles Henry McClennahan, the costume design was by Daphne Pascucci, the lighting design was by Peter Maradudin; the music director was Dwight Andrews. The cast was as follows:

STURDYVANT	John Carpenter
IRVIN	Lou Criscuolo
CUTLER	Joe Seneca
TOLEDO	Robert Judd
SLOW DRAG	Leonard Jackson
LEVEE	Charles S. Dutton
MA RAINEY	Theresa Merritt
POLICEMAN	Christopher Loomis
DUSSIE MAE	Aleta Mitchell
SYLVESTER	Scott Davenport-Richards

CHARACTERS

STURDYVANT

IRVIN

CUTLER

TOLEDO

SLOW DRAG

LEVEE

MA RAINEY

POLICEMAN

DUSSIE MAE

SYLVESTER

SETTING

There are two playing areas: what is called the "band room,"
and the recording studio. The band room is at stage left and is
in the basement of the building. It is entered through a door
up left. There are benches and chairs scattered about, a piano,
a row of lockers, and miscellaneous paraphernalia stacked in a
corner and long since forgotten. A mirror hangs on a wall with
various posters.

The studio is upstairs at stage right, and resembles a
recording studio of the late 1920s. The entrance is from a hall
on the right wall. A small control booth is at the rear and its
access is gained by means of a spiral staircase. Against one wall

there is a line of chairs, and a horn through which the control room communicates with the performers. A door in the rear wall allows access to the band room.

THE PLAY

It is early March in Chicago, 1927. There is a bit of a chill in the air. Winter has broken but the wind coming off the lake does not carry the promise of spring. The people of the city are bundled and brisk in their defense against such misfortunes as the weather, and the business of the city proceeds largely undisturbed.

Chicago in 1927 is a rough city, a bruising city, a city of millionaires and derelicts, gangsters and roughhouse dandies, whores and Irish grandmothers who move through its streets fingering long black rosaries. Somewhere a man is wrestling with the taste of a woman in his cheek. Somewhere a dog is barking. Somewhere the moon has fallen through a window and broken into thirty pieces of silver.

It is one o'clock in the afternoon. Secretaries are returning from their lunch, the noon Mass at Saint Anthony's is over, and the priest is mumbling over his vestments while the altar boys practice their Latin. The procession of cattle cars through the stockyards continues unabated. The busboys in Mac's Place are cleaning away the last of the corned beef and cabbage, and on the city's Southside, sleepy-eyed Negroes move lazily toward their small cold-water flats and rented rooms to await the onslaught of night, which will find them crowded in the bars and juke joints both dazed and dazzling in their rapport with life. It is with these Negroes that our concern lies most heavily: their values, their attitudes, and particularly their music.

It is hard to define this music. Suffice it to say that it is music that breathes and touches. That connects. That is in itself a way of being, separate and distinct from any other. This music is called blues. Whether this music came from

Alabama or Mississippi or other parts of the South doesn't matter anymore. The men and women who make this music have learned it from the narrow crooked streets of East St. Louis, or the streets of the city's Southside, and the Alabama or Mississippi roots have been strangled by the Northern manners and customs of free men of definite and sincere worth, men for whom this music often lies at the forefront of their conscience and concerns. Thus they are laid open to be consumed by it; its warmth and redress, its braggadocio and roughly poignant comments, its vision and prayer, which would instruct and allow them to reconnect, to reassemble and gird up for the next battle in which they would be both victim and the ten thousand slain.

They tore the railroad down
so the Sunshine Special can't run
I'm going away baby
build me a railroad of my own.

—BLIND LEMON JEFFERSON

ACT ONE

The lights come up in the studio. Irvin enters, carrying a microphone. He is a tall, fleshy man who prides himself on his knowledge of blacks and his ability to deal with them. He hooks up the microphone, blows into it, taps it, etc. He crosses over to the piano, opens it, and fingers a few keys. Sturdyvant is visible in the control booth. Preoccupied with money, he is insensitive to black performers and prefers to deal with them at arm's length. He puts on a pair of earphones.

STURDYVANT (*Over speaker*): Irv . . . let's crack that mike, huh? Let's do a check on it.

IRVIN (*Crosses to mike, speaks into it*): Testing . . . one . . . two . . . three . . . (*There is a loud feedback. Sturdyvant fiddles with the dials*) Testing . . . one . . . two . . . three . . . testing. How's that, Mel? (*Sturdyvant doesn't respond*) Testing . . . one . . . two . . .

STURDYVANT (*Taking off earphones*): Okay . . . that checks. We got a good reading. (*Pause*) You got that list, Irv?

IRVIN: Yeah . . . yeah, I got it. Don't worry about nothing.

9

STURDYVANT: Listen, Irv . . . you keep her in line, okay? I'm holding you responsible for her . . . If she starts any of her . . .

IRVIN: Mel, what's with the goddamn horn? You wanna talk to me . . . okay! I can't talk to you over the goddamn horn . . . Christ!

STURDYVANT: I'm not putting up with any shenanigans. You hear, Irv?

(Irvin crosses over to the piano and mindlessly runs his fingers over the keys.)

I'm just not gonna stand for it. I want you to keep her in line. Irv?

(Sturdyvant enters from the control booth.)

Listen, Irv . . . you're her manager . . . she's your responsibility . . .

IRVIN: Okay, okay, Mel . . . let me handle it.

STURDYVANT: She's your responsibility. I'm not putting up with any Royal Highness . . . Queen of the Blues bullshit!

IRVIN: Mother of the Blues, Mel. Mother of the Blues.

STURDYVANT: I don't care what she calls herself. I'm not putting up with it. I just want to get her in here . . . record those songs on that list . . . and get her out. Just like clockwork, huh?

IRVIN: Like clockwork, Mel. You just stay out of the way and let me handle it.

STURDYVANT: Yeah . . . yeah . . . you handled it last time. Remember? She marches in here like she owns the damn place . . . doesn't like the songs we picked out . . . says her throat is sore . . . doesn't want to do more than one take . . .

IRVIN: Okay . . . okay . . . I was here! I know all about it.

STURDYVANT: Complains about the building being cold . . . and then . . . trips over the mike wire and threatens to sue me. That's taking care of it?

IRVIN: I've got it all worked out this time. I talked with her last night. Her throat is fine . . . We went over the songs together . . . I got everything straight, Mel.

STURDYVANT: Irv, that horn player . . . the one who gave me those songs . . . is he gonna be here today? Good. I want to hear more of that sound. Times are changing. This is a tricky business now. We've got to jazz it up . . . put in something different. You know, something wild . . . with a lot of rhythm. *(Pause)* You know what we put out last time, Irv? We put out garbage last time. It was garbage. I don't even know why I bother with this anymore.

IRVIN: You did all right last time, Mel. Not as good as you did before, but you did all right.

STURDYVANT: You know how many records we sold in New York? You wanna see the sheet? And you know what's in New York, Irv? Harlem. Harlem's in New York, Irv.

IRVIN: Okay, so they didn't sell in New York. But look at Memphis . . . Birmingham . . . Atlanta. Christ, you made a bundle.

STURDYVANT: It's not the money, Irv. You know I couldn't sleep last night? This business is bad for my nerves. My wife is after me to slow down and take a vacation. Two more years and I'm gonna get out . . . get into something respectable. Textiles. That's a respectable business. You know what you could do with a shipload of textiles from Ireland?

(A buzzer is heard offstage.)

IRVIN: Why don't you go upstairs and let me handle it, Mel?

STURDYVANT: Remember . . . you're responsible for her.

(Sturdyvant exits to the control booth. Irvin crosses to get the door. Cutler, Slow Drag and Toledo enter. Cutler is in his mid-fifties, as are most of the others. He plays guitar and trombone and is the leader of the group, possibly because he is the most sensible. His playing is solid and almost totally unembellished. His understanding of his music is limited to the chord he is playing at the time he is playing it. He has all the qualities of a loner except the introspection. Slow Drag, the bass player, is perhaps the one most bored by life. He resembles Cutler, but lacks Cutler's energy. He is deceptively intelligent, though, as his name implies, he appears to be slow. He is a rather large man with a wicked smile. Innate African rhythms underlie everything he plays, and he plays with an ease that is at times startling. Toledo is the piano player. In control of his instrument, he understands and recognizes that its limitations are an extension of himself. He is the only one in the group who can read. He is self-taught but misunderstands and misapplies his knowledge, though he is quick to penetrate to the core of a situation and his insights are thought-provoking. All of the men are dressed in a style of clothing befitting the members of a successful band of the era.)

IRVIN: How you boys doing, Cutler? Come on in. *(Pause)* Where's Ma? Is she with you?

CUTLER: I don't know, Mr. Irvin. She told us to be here at one o'clock. That's all I know.

IRVIN: Where's . . . huh . . . the horn player? Is he coming with Ma?

CUTLER: Levee's supposed to be here same as we is. I reckon he'll be here in a minute. I can't rightly say.

IRVIN: Well, come on . . . I'll show you to the band room, let you get set up and rehearsed. You boys hungry? I'll call over to the deli and get some sandwiches. Get you fed and ready to make some music. Cutler . . . here's the list of songs we're gonna record.

STURDYVANT *(Over speaker)*: Irvin, what's happening? Where's Ma?

IRVIN: Everything under control, Mel. I got it under control.

STURDYVANT: Where's Ma? How come she isn't with the band?

IRVIN: She'll be here in a minute, Mel. Let me get these fellows down to the band room, huh?

(They exit the studio. The lights go down in the studio and up in the band room. Irvin opens the door and allows them to pass as they enter.)

You boys go ahead and rehearse. I'll let you know when Ma comes.

(Irvin exits. Cutler hands Toledo the list of songs.)

CUTLER: What we got here, Toledo?

TOLEDO *(Reading)*: We got . . . "Prove It on Me" . . . "Hear Me Talking to You" . . . "Ma Rainey's Black Bottom" . . . and "Moonshine Blues."

CUTLER: Where Mr. Irvin go? Them ain't the songs Ma told me.

SLOW DRAG: I wouldn't worry about it if I were you, Cutler. They'll get it straightened out. Ma will get it straightened out.

CUTLER: I just don't want no trouble about these songs, that's all. Ma ain't told me them songs. She told me something else.

SLOW DRAG: What she tell you?

CUTLER: This "Moonshine Blues" wasn't in it. That's one of Bessie's songs.

TOLEDO: Slow Drag's right . . . I wouldn't worry about it. Let them straighten it up.

CUTLER: Levee know what time he supposed to be here?

SLOW DRAG: Levee gone out to spend your four dollars. He left the hotel this morning talking about he was gonna go buy some shoes. Say it's the first time he ever beat you shooting craps.

CUTLER: Do he know what time he supposed to be here? That's what I wanna know. I ain't thinking about no four dollars.

SLOW DRAG: Levee sure was thinking about it. That four dollars liked to burn a hole in his pocket.

CUTLER: Well, he's supposed to be here at one o'clock. That's what time Ma said. That nigger get out in the streets with that four dollars and ain't no telling when he's liable to show. You ought to have seen him at the club last night, Toledo. Trying to talk to some gal Ma had with her.

TOLEDO: You ain't got to tell me. I know how Levee do.

(Buzzer is heard offstage.)

SLOW DRAG: Levee tried to talk to that gal and got his feelings hurt. She didn't want no part of him. She told Levee he'd have to turn his money green before he could talk with her.

CUTLER: She out for what she can get. Anybody could see that.

SLOW DRAG: That's why Levee run out to buy some shoes. He's looking to make an impression on that gal.

CUTLER: What the hell she gonna do with his shoes? She can't do nothing with the nigger's shoes.

(Slow Drag takes out a pint bottle and drinks.)

TOLEDO: Let me hit that, Slow Drag.

SLOW DRAG *(Handing him the bottle)*: This some of that good Chicago bourbon!

(The door opens and Levee enters, carrying a shoe box. In his early thirties, Levee is younger than the other men. His flamboyance is sometimes subtle and sneaks up on you. His temper is rakish and bright. He lacks fuel for himself and is somewhat of a buffoon. But it is an intelligent buffoonery, clearly calculated to shift

control of the situation to where he can grasp it. He plays trumpet. His voice is strident and totally dependent on his manipulation of breath. He plays wrong notes frequently. He often gets his skill and talent confused with each other.)

CUTLER: Levee . . . where Mr. Irvin go?

LEVEE: Hell, I don't know. I ain't none of his keeper.

SLOW DRAG: What you got there, Levee?

LEVEE: Look here, Cutler . . . I got me some shoes!

CUTLER: Nigger, I ain't studying you.

(Levee takes the shoes out of the box and starts to put them on.)

TOLEDO: How much you pay for something like that, Levee?

LEVEE: Eleven dollars. Four dollars of it belong to Cutler.

SLOW DRAG: Levee say if it wasn't for Cutler . . . he wouldn't have no new shoes.

CUTLER: I ain't thinking about Levee or his shoes. Come on . . . let's get ready to rehearse.

SLOW DRAG: I'm with you on that score, Cutler. I wanna get out of here. I don't want to be around here all night. When it comes time to go up there and record them songs . . . I just wanna go up there and do it. Last time it took us all day and half the night.

TOLEDO: Ain't but four songs on the list. Last time we recorded six songs.

SLOW DRAG: It felt like it was sixteen!

LEVEE *(Finishes with his shoes)*: Yeah! Now I'm ready! I can play some good music now! *(Goes to put up his old shoes and looks around the room)* Damn! They done changed things around. Don't never leave well enough alone.

TOLEDO: Everything changing all the time. Even the air you breathing change. You got, monoxide, hydrogen . . . changing all the time. Skin changing . . . different molecules and everything.

LEVEE: Nigger, what is you talking about? I'm talking about the room. I ain't talking about no skin and air. I'm talking about something I can see! Last time the band room was upstairs. This time it's downstairs. Next time it be over there. I'm talking about what I can see. I ain't talking about no molecules or nothing.

TOLEDO: Hell, I know what you talking about. I just said everything changin'. I know what you talking about, but you don't know what I'm talking about.

LEVEE: That door! Nigger, you see that door? That's what I'm talking about. That door wasn't there before.

CUTLER: Levee, you wouldn't know your right from your left. This is where they used to keep the recording horns and things . . . and damn if that door wasn't there. How in hell else you gonna get in here? Now, if you talking about they done switched rooms, you right. But don't go telling me that damn door wasn't there!

SLOW DRAG: Damn the door and let's get set up. I wanna get out of here.

LEVEE: Toledo started all that about the door. I'm just saying that things change.

TOLEDO: What the hell you think I was saying? Things change. The air and everything. Now you gonna say you was saying it. You gonna fit two propositions on the same track . . . run them into each other, and because they crash, you gonna say it's the same train.

LEVEE: Now this nigger talking about trains! We done went from the air to the skin to the door . . . and now trains. Toledo, I'd just like to be inside your head for five minutes. Just to see how you think. You done got more shit piled up and mixed up in there than the devil got sinners. You been reading too many goddamn books.

TOLEDO: What you care about how much I read? I'm gonna ignore you 'cause you ignorant.

(Levee takes off his coat and hangs it in the locker.)

SLOW DRAG: Come on, let's rehearse the music.

LEVEE: You ain't gotta rehearse that . . . ain't nothing but old jug-band music. They need one of them jug bands for this.

SLOW DRAG: Don't make me no difference. Long as we get paid.

LEVEE: That ain't what I'm talking about, nigger. I'm talking about art!

SLOW DRAG: What's drawing got to do with it?

LEVEE: Where you get this nigger from, Cutler? He sound like one of them Alabama niggers.

CUTLER: Slow Drag's all right. It's you talking all that weird shit about art. Just play the piece, nigger. You wanna be one of them . . . what you call . . . virtuoso or something, you in the wrong place. You ain't no Buddy Bolden or King Oliver . . . you just an old trumpet player come a dime a dozen. Talking about art.

LEVEE: What is you? I don't see your name in lights.

CUTLER: I just play the piece. Whatever they want. I don't go talking about art and criticizing other people's music.

LEVEE: I ain't like you, Cutler. I got talent! Me and this horn . . . we's tight. If my daddy knowed I was gonna turn out like this, he would've named me Gabriel. I'm gonna get me a band and make me some records. I done give Mr. Sturdyvant some of my songs I wrote and he say he's gonna let me record them when I get my band together. *(Takes some papers out of his pocket)* I just gotta finish the last part of this song. And Mr. Sturdyvant want me to write another part to this song.

SLOW DRAG: How you learn to write music, Levee?

LEVEE: I just picked it up . . . like you pick up anything. Miss Eula used to play the piano . . . she learned me a lot. I knows how to play *real* music . . . not this old jug-band shit. I got style!

TOLEDO: Everybody got style. Style ain't nothing but keeping the same idea from beginning to end. Everybody got it.

LEVEE: But everybody can't play like I do. Everybody can't have their own band.

CUTLER: Well, until you get your own band where you can play what you want, you just play the piece and stop complaining. I told you when you came on here, this ain't none of them hot bands. This is an accompaniment band. You play Ma's music when you here.

LEVEE: I got sense enough to know that. Hell, I can look at you all and see what kind of band it is. I can look at Toledo and see what kind of band it is.

TOLEDO: Toledo ain't said nothing to you now. Don't let Toledo get started. You can't even spell music, much less play it.

LEVEE: What you talking about? I can spell music. I got a dollar say I can spell it! Put your dollar up. Where your dollar?

(Toledo waves him away.)

Now come on. Put your dollar up. Talking about I can't spell music.

(Levee peels a dollar off his roll and slams it down on the bench beside Toledo.)

TOLEDO: All right, I'm gonna show you. Cutler. Slow Drag. You hear this? The nigger betting me a dollar he can spell music. I don't want no shit now! (Lays a dollar down beside Levee's) All right. Go ahead. Spell it.

LEVEE: It's a bet then. Talking about I can't spell music.

TOLEDO: Go ahead, then. Spell it. Music. Spell it.

LEVEE: I can spell it, nigger! M-U-S-I-K. There! (Reaches for the money)

TOLEDO: Naw! Naw! Leave that money alone! You ain't
spelled it.

LEVEE: What you mean I ain't spelled it? I said M-U-S-I-K!

TOLEDO: That ain't how you spell it! That ain't how you spell
it! It's M-U-S-I-C! C, nigger. Not K! C! M-U-S-I-C!

LEVEE: What you mean, C? Who say it's C?

TOLEDO: Cutler. Slow Drag. Tell this fool.

(They look at each other and then away.)

Well, I'll be a monkey's uncle!

(Toledo picks up the money and hands Levee his dollar back.)

Here's your dollar back, Levee. I done won it, you understand. I done won the dollar. But if don't nobody know
but me, how am I gonna prove it to you?

LEVEE: You just mad 'cause I spelled it.

TOLEDO: Spelled what! M-U-S-I-K don't spell nothing. I just
wish there was some way I could show you the right and
wrong of it. How you gonna know something if the other
fellow don't know if you're right or not? Now I can't even
be sure that I'm spelling it right.

LEVEE: That's what I'm talking about. You don't know it.
Talking about C. You ought to give me that dollar I won
from you.

TOLEDO: All right. All right. I'm gonna show you how ridiculous you sound. You know the Lord's Prayer?

LEVEE: Why? You wanna bet a dollar on that?

TOLEDO: Just answer the question. Do you know the Lord's
Prayer or don't you?

LEVEE: Yeah, I know it. What of it?

TOLEDO: Cutler?

CUTLER: What you Cutlering me for? I ain't got nothing to do
with it.

TOLEDO: I just want to show the man how ridiculous he is.

CUTLER: Both of you all sound like damn fools. Arguing about something silly. Yeah, I know the Lord's Prayer. My daddy was a deacon in the church. Come asking me if I know the Lord's Prayer. Yeah, I know it.

TOLEDO: Slow Drag?

SLOW DRAG: Yeah.

TOLEDO: All right. Now I'm gonna tell you a story to show just how ridiculous he sound. There was these two fellows, see. So, the one of them go up to this church and commence to taking up the church learning. The other fellow see him out on the road and he say, "I done heard you taking up the church learning," say, "Is you learning anything up there?" The other one say, "Yeah, I done take up the church learning and I's learning all kinds of things about the Bible and what it say and all. Why you be asking?" The other one say, "Well, do you know the Lord's Prayer?" And he say, "Why, sure I know the Lord's Prayer, I'm taking up learning at the church, ain't I? I know the Lord's Prayer backwards and forwards." And the other fellow says, "I bet you five dollars you don't know the Lord's Prayer, 'cause I don't think you knows it. I think you be going up to the church 'cause the Widow Jenkins be going up there and you just wanna be sitting in the same room with her when she cross them big, fine, pretty legs she got." And the other one say, "Well, I'm gonna prove you wrong and I'm gonna bet you that five dollars." So he say, "Well, go on and say it then." So he commenced to saying the Lord's Prayer. He say, "Now I lay me down to sleep, I pray the Lord my soul to keep." The other one say, "Here's your five dollars. I didn't think you knew it." (They all laugh) Now, that's just how ridiculous Levee sound. Only 'cause I knowed how to spell music, I still got my dollar.

LEVEE: That don't prove nothing. What's that supposed to prove?

(Toledo takes a newspaper out of his back pocket and begins to read.)

TOLEDO: I'm through with it.

SLOW DRAG: Is you all gonna rehearse this music or ain't you?

(Cutler takes out some papers and starts to roll a reefer.)

LEVEE: How many times you done played them songs? What you gotta rehearse for?

SLOW DRAG: This a recording session. I wanna get it right the first time and get on out of here.

CUTLER: Slow Drag's right. Let's go on and rehearse and get it over with.

LEVEE: You all go and rehearse, then. I got to finish this song for Mr. Sturdyvant.

CUTLER: Come on, Levee . . . I don't want no shit now. You rehearse like everybody else. You in the band like everybody else. Mr. Sturdyvant just gonna have to wait. You got to do that on your own time. This is the band's time.

LEVEE: Well, what is you doing? You sitting there rolling a reefer talking about let's rehearse. Toledo reading a newspaper. Hell, I'm ready if you wanna rehearse. I just say there ain't no point in it. Ma ain't here. What's the point in it?

CUTLER: Nigger, why you gotta complain all the time?

TOLEDO: Levee would complain if a gal ain't laid across his bed just right.

CUTLER: That's what I know. That's why I try to tell him just play the music and forget about it. It ain't no big thing.

TOLEDO: Levee ain't got an eye for that. He wants to tie on to some abstract component and sit down on the elemental.

LEVEE: This is get-on-Levee time, huh? Levee ain't said nothing except this some old jug-band music.

TOLEDO: Under the right circumstances you'd play anything. If you know music, then you play it. Straight on or off to the side. Ain't nothing abstract about it.

LEVEE: Toledo, you sound like you got a mouth full of mar-
bles. You the only cracker-talking nigger I know.

TOLEDO: You ought to have learned yourself to read . . . then
you'd understand the basic understanding of everything.

SLOW DRAG: Both of you all gonna drive me crazy with that
philosophy bullshit. Cutler, give me a reefer.

CUTLER: Ain't you got some reefer? Where's your reefer? Why
you all the time asking me?

SLOW DRAG: Cutler, how long I done known you? How long
we been together? Twenty-two years. We been doing this
together for twenty-two years. All up and down the back
roads, the side roads, the front roads . . . We done played
the juke joints, the whorehouses, the barn dances, and city
sit-downs . . . I done lied for you and lied with you . . . We
done laughed together, fought together, slept in the same
bed together, done sucked on the same titty . . . and now
you don't wanna give me no reefer.

CUTLER: You see this nigger trying to talk me out of my reefer,
Toledo? Running all that about how long he done knowed
me and how we done sucked on the same titty. Nigger, you
still ain't getting none of my reefer!

TOLEDO: That's African.

SLOW DRAG: What? What you talking about? What's African?

LEVEE: I know he ain't talking about me. You don't see me running around in no jungle with no bone between my nose.

TOLEDO: Levee, you worse than ignorant. You ignorant without a premise. (*Pause*) Now, what I was saying is what Slow
Drag was doing is African. That's what you call an African
conceptualization. That's when you name the gods or call on
the ancestors to achieve whatever your desires are.

SLOW DRAG: Nigger, I ain't no African! I ain't doing no African nothing!

TOLEDO: Naming all those things you and Cutler done together
is like trying to solicit some reefer based on a bond of kin-

ship. That's African. An ancestral retention. Only you forgot the name of the gods.

SLOW DRAG: I ain't forgot nothing. I was telling the nigger
how cheap he is. Don't come talking that African nonsense to me.

TOLEDO: You just like Levee. No eye for taking an abstract
and fixing it to a specific. There's so much that goes on
around you and you can't even see it.

CUTLER: Wait a minute . . . wait a minute. Toledo, now when
this nigger . . . when an African do all them things you say
and name all the gods and whatnot . . . then what happens?

TOLEDO: Depends on if the gods is sympathetic with his cause
for which he is calling them with the right names. Then
his success comes with the right proportion of his naming.
That's the way that go.

CUTLER (*Taking out a reefer*): Here, Slow Drag. Here's a reefer.
You done talked yourself up on that one.

SLOW DRAG: Thank you. You ought to have done that in the
first place and saved me all the aggravation.

CUTLER: What I wants to know is . . . what's the same titty we
done sucked on. That's what I want to know.

SLOW DRAG: Oh, I just threw that in there to make it sound
good.

(*They all laugh.*)

CUTLER: Nigger, you ain't right.

SLOW DRAG: I knows it.

CUTLER: Well, come on . . . let's get it rehearsed. Time's wasting.

(*The musicians pick up their instruments.*)

Let's do it. "Ma Rainey's Black Bottom." One . . . two . . .
You know what to do.

(They begin to play. Levee is playing something different. He stops.)

LEVEE: Naw! Naw! We ain't doing it that way.

(Toledo stops playing, then Slow Drag.)

We doing my version. It say so right there on that piece of paper you got. Ask Toledo. That's what Mr. Irvin told me . . . say it's on the list he gave you.

CUTLER: Let me worry about what's on the list and what ain't on the list. How you gonna tell me what's on the list?

LEVEE: 'Cause I know what Mr. Irvin told me! Ask Toledo!

CUTLER: Let me worry about what's on the list. You just play the song I say.

LEVEE: What kind of sense it make to rehearse the wrong version of the song? That's what I wanna know. Why you wanna rehearse that version?

SLOW DRAG: You supposed to rehearse what you gonna play. That's the way they taught me. Now, *whatever* version we gonna play . . . let's go on and rehearse it.

LEVEE: That's what I'm trying to tell the man.

CUTLER: You trying to tell me what we is and ain't gonna play. And that ain't none of your business. Your business is to play what I say.

LEVEE: Oh, I see now. You done got jealous 'cause Mr. Irvin using my version. You done got jealous 'cause I proved I know something about music.

CUTLER: What the hell . . . nigger, you talk like a fool! What the hell I got to be jealous of you about? The day I get jealous of you I may as well lay down and die.

TOLEDO: Levee started all that 'cause he too lazy to rehearse. *(To Levee)* You ought to just go on and play the song . . . What difference does it make?

LEVEE: Where's the paper? Look at the paper! Get the paper and look at it! See what it say. Gonna tell me I'm too lazy to rehearse.

CUTLER: We ain't talking about the paper. We talking about you understanding where you fit in when you around here. You just play what I say.

LEVEE: Look . . . I don't care what you play! All right? It don't matter to me. Mr. Irvin gonna straighten it up! I don't care what you play.

CUTLER: Thank you. (*Pause*) Let's play this "Hear Me Talking to You" till we find out what's happening with the "Black Bottom." Slow Drag, you sing Ma's part. (*Pause*) "Hear Me Talking to You." Let's do it. One . . . two . . . You know what to do.

(*They play.*)

SLOW DRAG (*Singing*):
> Rambling man makes no change in me
> I'm gonna ramble back to my used-to-be
> Ah, you hear me talking to you
> I don't bite my tongue
> You wants to be my man
> You got to fetch it with you when you come.

> Eve and Adam in the garden taking a chance
> Adam didn't take time to get his pants
> Ah, you hear me talking to you
> I don't bite my tongue
> You wants to be my man
> You got to fetch it with you when you come.

> Our old cat swallowed a ball of yarn
> When the kittens were born they had sweaters on
> Ah, you hear me talking to you

I don't bite my tongue
You wants to be my man
You got to fetch it with you when you come.

(Irvin enters. The musicians stop playing.)

IRVIN: Any of you boys know what's keeping Ma?
CUTLER: Can't say, Mr. Irvin. She'll be along directly, I reckon. I talked to her this morning, she say she'll be here in time to rehearse.
IRVIN: Well, you boys go ahead. *(Starts to exit)*
CUTLER: Mr. Irvin, about these songs . . . Levee say . . .
IRVIN: Whatever's on the list, Cutler. You got that list I gave you?
CUTLER: Yessir, I got it right here.
IRVIN: Whatever's on there. Whatever that says.
CUTLER: I'm asking about this "Black Bottom" piece . . . Levee say . . .
IRVIN: Oh, it's on the list. "Ma Rainey's Black Bottom" on the list.
CUTLER: I know it's on the list. I wanna know what version. We got two versions of that song.
IRVIN: Oh. Levee's arrangement. We're using Levee's arrangement.
CUTLER: Okay. I got that straight. Now, this "Moonshine Blues" . . .
IRVIN: We'll work it out with Ma, Cutler. Just rehearse whatever's on the list and use Levee's arrangement on that "Black Bottom" piece. *(Exits)*
LEVEE: See, I told you! It don't mean nothing when I say it. You got to wait for Mr. Irvin to say it. Well, I told you the way it is.
CUTLER: Levee, the sooner you understand it ain't what you say, or what Mr. Irvin say . . . it's what Ma say that counts.
SLOW DRAG: Don't nobody say when it come to Ma. She's gonna do what she wants to do. Ma says what happens with her.

LEVEE: Hell, the man's the one putting out the record! He's gonna put out what he wanna put out!

SLOW DRAG: He's gonna put out what Ma want him to put out.

LEVEE: You heard what the man told you . . . "Ma Rainey's Black Bottom," Levee's arrangement. There you go! That's what he told you.

SLOW DRAG: What you gonna do, Cutler?

CUTLER: Ma ain't told me what version. Let's go on and play it Levee's way.

TOLEDO: See, now . . . I'll tell you something. As long as the colored man look to white folks to put the crown on what he say . . . as long as he looks to white folks for approval . . . then he ain't never gonna find out who he is and what he's about. He's just gonna be about what white folks want him to be about. That's one sure thing.

LEVEE: I'm just trying to show Cutler where he's wrong.

CUTLER: Cutler don't need you to show him nothing.

SLOW DRAG (Irritated): Come on, let's get this shit rehearsed! You all can bicker afterward!

CUTLER: Levee's confused about who the boss is. He don't know Ma's the boss.

LEVEE: Ma's the boss on the road! We at a recording session. Mr. Sturdyvant and Mr. Irvin say what's gonna be here! We's in Chicago, we ain't in Memphis! I don't know why you all wanna pick me about it, shit! I'm with Slow Drag . . . Let's go on and get it rehearsed.

CUTLER: All right. All right. I know how to solve this. "Ma Rainey's Black Bottom." Levee's version. Let's do it. Come on.

TOLEDO: How that first part go again, Levee?

LEVEE: It go like this. (Plays) That's to get the people's attention to the song. That's when you and Slow Drag come in with the rhythm part. Me and Cutler play on the breaks. (Becoming animated) Now we gonna dance it . . . but we ain't gonna countrify it. This ain't no barn dance. We gonna play it like—

CUTLER: The man ask you how the first part go. He don't wanna hear all that. Just tell him how the piece go.

TOLEDO: I got it. I got it. Let's go. I know how to do it.

CUTLER: "Ma Rainey's Black Bottom." One . . . two . . . You know what to do.

(They begin to play. Levee stops.)

LEVEE: You all got to keep up now. You playing in the wrong time. Ma come in over the top. She got to find her own way in.

CUTLER: Nigger, will you let us play this song? When you get your own band . . . then you tell them that nonsense. We know how to play the piece. I was playing music before you was born. Gonna tell me how to play . . . All right. Let's try it again.

SLOW DRAG: Cutler, wait till I fix this. This string started to unravel. *(Playfully)* And you know I want to play Levee's music right.

LEVEE: If you was any kind of musician, you'd take care of your instrument. Keep it in tip-top order. If you was any kind of musician, I'd let you be in my band.

SLOW DRAG: Shhheeeeet!

(Slow Drag crosses to get his string and steps on Levee's shoes.)

LEVEE: Damn, Slow Drag! Watch them big-ass shoes you got.

SLOW DRAG: Boy, ain't nobody done nothing to you.

LEVEE: You done stepped on my shoes.

SLOW DRAG: Move them the hell out the way, then. You was in my way . . . I wasn't in your way.

(Cutler lights up another reefer. Slow Drag rummages around in his belongings for a string. Levee takes out a rag and begins to shine his shoes.)

You can shine these when you get done, Levee.

CUTLER: If I had them shoes Levee got, I could buy me a whole suit of clothes.

LEVEE: What kind of difference it make what kind of shoes I got? Ain't nothing wrong with having nice shoes. I ain't said nothing about your shoes. Why you wanna talk about me and my Florsheim's?

CUTLER: Any man who takes a whole week's pay and puts it on some shoes—you understand what I mean, what you walk around on the ground with—is a fool! And I don't mind telling you.

LEVEE (Irritated): What difference it make to you, Cutler?

SLOW DRAG: The man ain't said nothing about your shoes. Ain't nothing wrong with having nice shoes. Look at Toledo.

TOLEDO: What about Toledo?

SLOW DRAG: I said ain't nothing wrong with having nice shoes.

LEVEE: Nigger got them clodhoppers! Old brogans! He ain't nothing but a sharecropper.

TOLEDO: You can make all the fun you want. It don't mean nothing. I'm satisfied with them and that's what counts.

LEVEE: Nigger, why don't you get some decent shoes? Got nerve to put on a suit and tie with them farming boots.

CUTLER: What you just tell me? It don't make no difference about the man's shoes. That's what you told me.

LEVEE: Aw, hell, I don't care what the nigger wear. I'll be honest with you. I don't care if he went barefoot.

(Slow Drag has put his string on the bass and is tuning it.)

Play something for me, Slow Drag.

(Slow Drag plays.)

A man got to have some shoes to dance like this! You can't dance like this with them clodhoppers Toledo got. (Singing:)

Hello Central give me Doctor Jazz
He's got just what I need I'll say he has
When the world goes wrong and I have got the blues
He's the man who makes me get on my dancing shoes.

TOLEDO: That's the trouble with colored folks . . . always wanna have a good time. Good times done got more niggers killed than God got ways to count. What the hell having a good time mean? That's what I wanna know.

LEVEE: Hell, nigger . . . it don't need explaining. Ain't you never had no good time before?

TOLEDO: The more niggers get killed having a good time, the more good times niggers wanna have.

(Slow Drag stops playing.)

There's more to life than having a good time. If there ain't, then this is a piss-poor life we're having . . . if that's all there is to be got out of it.

SLOW DRAG: Toledo, just 'cause you like to read them books and study and whatnot . . . that's your good time. People get other things they likes to do to have a good time. Ain't no need you picking them about it.

CUTLER: Niggers been having a good time before you was born, and they gonna keep having a good time after you gone.

TOLEDO: Yeah, but what else they gonna do? Ain't nobody talking about making the lot of the colored man better for him here in America.

LEVEE: Now you gonna be Booker T. Washington.

TOLEDO: Everybody worried about having a good time. Ain't nobody thinking about what kind of world they gonna leave their youngens. "Just give me the good time, that's all I want." It just makes me sick.

SLOW DRAG: Well, the colored man's gonna be all right. He got through slavery, and he'll get through whatever else the white man put on him. I ain't worried about that. Good times is what makes life worth living. Now, you take the white man . . . The white man don't know how to have a good time. That's why he's troubled all the time. He don't know how to have a good time. He don't know how to laugh at life.

LEVEE: That's what the problem is with Toledo . . . reading all them books and things. He done got to the point where he forgot how to laugh and have a good time. Just like the white man.

TOLEDO: I know how to have a good time as well as the next man. I said, there's got to be more to life than having a good time. I said the colored man ought to be doing more than just trying to have a good time all the time.

LEVEE: Well, what is you doing, nigger? Talking all them high-falutin ideas about making a better world for the colored man. What is you doing to make it better? You playing the music and looking for your next piece of pussy same as we is. What is you doing? That's what I wanna know. Tell him, Cutler.

CUTLER: You all leave Cutler out of this. Cutler ain't got nothing to do with it.

TOLEDO: Levee, you just about the most ignorant nigger I know. Sometimes I wonder why I ever bother to try and talk with you.

LEVEE: Well, what is you doing? Talking that shit to me about I'm ignorant! What is you doing? You just a whole lot of mouth. A great big windbag. Thinking you smarter than everybody else. What is you doing, huh?

TOLEDO: It ain't just me, fool! It's everybody! What you think . . . I'm gonna solve the colored man's problems by myself? I said, we. You understand that? We. That's every living colored man in the world got to do his share. Got to do his part. I ain't talking about what I'm gonna do . . . or what you or Cutler or Slow Drag or anybody else. I'm talking about all of us together. What all of us is gonna do. That's what I'm talking about, nigger!

LEVEE: Well, why didn't you say that, then?

CUTLER: Toledo, I don't know why you waste your time on this fool.

TOLEDO: That's what I'm trying to figure out.

LEVEE: Now there go Cutler with his shit. Calling me a fool. You wasn't even in the conversation. Now you gonna take sides and call me a fool.

CUTLER: Hell, I was listening to the man. I got sense enough to know what he was saying. I could tell it straight back to you.

LEVEE: Well, you go on with it. But I'll tell you this . . . I ain't gonna be too many more of your fools. I'll tell you that. Now you put that in your pipe and smoke it.

CUTLER: Boy, ain't nobody studying you. Telling me what to put in my pipe. Who's you to tell me what to do?

LEVEE: All right, I ain't nobody. Don't pay me no mind. I ain't nobody.

TOLEDO: Levee, you ain't nothing but the devil.

LEVEE: There you go! That's who I am. I'm the devil. I ain't nothing but the devil.

CUTLER: I can see that. That's something you know about. You know all about the devil.

LEVEE: I ain't saying what I know. I know plenty. What you know about the devil? Telling me what I know. What you know?

SLOW DRAG: I know a man sold his soul to the devil.

LEVEE: There you go! That's the only thing I ask about the devil . . . to see him coming so I can sell him this one I got. 'Cause if there's a God up there, he done went to sleep.

SLOW DRAG: Sold his soul to the devil himself. Name of Eliza Cottor. Lived in Tuscaloosa County, Alabama. The devil came by and he done upped and sold him his soul.

CUTLER: How you know the man done sold his soul to the devil, nigger? You talking that old-woman foolishness.

SLOW DRAG: Everybody know. It wasn't no secret. He went around working for the devil and everybody knowed it. Carried him a bag . . . one of them carpetbags. Folks say he carried the devil's papers and whatnot where he put your fingerprint on the paper with blood.

LEVEE: Where he at now? That's what I want to know. He can put my whole handprint if he want to!

CUTLER: That's the damnedest thing I ever heard! Folks kill me with that talk.

TOLEDO: Oh, that's real enough, all right. Some folks go arm in arm with the devil, shoulder to shoulder, and talk to him all the time. That's real, ain't nothing wrong in believing that.

SLOW DRAG: That's what I'm saying. Eliza Cotter is one of them. All right. The man living up in an old shack on Ben Foster's place, shoeing mules and horses, making them charms and things in secret. He done hooked up with the devil, showed up one day all fancied out with just the finest clothes you ever seen on a colored man . . . dressed just like one of them crackers . . . and carrying this bag with them papers and things. All right. Had a pocketful of money, just living the life of a rich man. Ain't done no more work or nothing. Just had him a string of women he run around with and throw his money away on. Bought him a big fine house . . . Well, it wasn't all that big, but it did have one of them white picket fences around it. Used to hire a man once a week just to paint that fence. Messed around there and one of the fellows of them gals he was messing with got fixed on him wrong and Eliza killed him. And he laughed about it. Sheriff come and arrest him, and then let him go. And he went around in that town laughing about killing this fellow. Trial come up, and the judge cut him loose. He must have been in converse with the devil too . . . 'cause he cut him loose and give him a bottle of whiskey! Folks ask what done happened to make him change, and he'd tell them straight out he done sold his soul to the devil and ask them if they wanted to sell theirs 'cause he could arrange it for them. Preacher see him coming, used to cross on the other side of the road. He'd just stand there and laugh at the preacher and call him a fool to his face.

CUTLER: Well, whatever happened to this fellow? What come of him? A man who, as you say, done sold his soul to the devil is bound to come to a bad end.

TOLEDO: I don't know about that. The devil's strong. The devil ain't no pushover.

SLOW DRAG: Oh, the devil had him under his wing, all right. Took good care of him. He ain't wanted for nothing.

CUTLER: What happened to him? That's what I want to know.

SLOW DRAG: Last I heard, he headed North with that bag of his, handing out hundred-dollar bills on the spot to whoever wanted to sign on with the devil. That's what I hear tell of him.

CUTLER: That's a bunch of fool talk. I don't know how you fix your mouth to tell that story. I don't believe that.

SLOW DRAG: I ain't asking you to believe it. I'm just telling you the facts of it.

LEVEE: I sure wish I knew where he went. He wouldn't have to convince me long. Hell, I'd even help him sign people up.

CUTLER: Nigger, God's gonna strike you down with that blasphemy you talking.

LEVEE: Oh, shit! God don't mean nothing to me. Let him strike me! Here I am, standing right here. What you talking about he's gonna strike me? Here I am! Let him strike me! I ain't scared of him. Talking that stuff to me.

CUTLER: All right. You gonna be sorry. You gonna fix yourself to have bad luck. Ain't nothing gonna work for you.

(*Buzzer sounds offstage.*)

LEVEE: Bad luck? What I care about some bad luck? You talking simple. I ain't knowed nothing but bad luck all my life. Couldn't get no worse. What the hell I care about some bad luck? Hell, I eat it every day for breakfast! You dumber than I thought you was . . . talking about bad luck.

CUTLER: All right, nigger, you'll see! Can't tell a fool nothing. You'll see!

(Irvin enters the studio, checks his watch, and calls down the stairs.)

IRVIN: Cutler . . . you boys' sandwiches are up here . . . Cutler?

CUTLER: Yessir, Mr. Irvin . . . be right there.

TOLEDO: I'll walk up there and get them.

(Toledo exits. The lights go down in the band room and up in the studio. Irvin paces back and forth in an agitated manner. Sturdyvant enters.)

STURDYVANT: Irv, what's happening? Is she here yet? Was that her?

IRVIN: It's the sandwiches, Mel. I told you . . . I'll let you know when she comes, huh?

STURDYVANT: What's keeping her? Do you know what time it is? Have you looked at the clock? You told me she'd be here. You told me you'd take care of it.

IRVIN: Mel, for Chrissakes! What do you want from me? What do you want me to do?

STURDYVANT: Look what time it is, Irv. You told me she'd be here.

IRVIN: She'll be here, okay? I don't know what's keeping her. You know they're always late, Mel.

STURDYVANT: You should have went by the hotel and made sure she was on time. You should have taken care of this. That's what you told me, huh? "I'll take care of it."

IRVIN: Okay! Okay! I didn't go by the hotel! What do you want me to do? She'll be here, okay? The band's here . . . she'll be here.

STURDYVANT: Okay, Irv. I'll take your word. But if she doesn't come . . . if she doesn't come . . .

(*Sturdyvant exits to the control booth as Toledo enters.*)

TOLEDO: Mr. Irvin . . . I come up to get the sandwiches.

IRVIN: Say . . . uh . . . look . . . one o'clock, right? She said one o'clock.

TOLEDO: That's what time she told us. Say be here at one o'clock.

IRVIN: Do you know what's keeping her? Do you know why she ain't here?

TOLEDO: I can't say, Mr. Irvin. Told us one o'clock.

(*The buzzer sounds. Irvin goes to the door. There is a flurry of commotion as Ma Rainey enters, followed closely by the Policeman, Dussie Mae and Sylvester. Ma Rainey is a short, heavy woman. She is dressed in a full-length fur coat with matching hat, an emerald-green dress, and several strands of pearls of varying lengths. Her hair is secured by a headband that matches her dress. Her manner is simple and direct, and she carries herself in a royal fashion. Dussie Mae is a young, dark-skinned woman whose greatest asset is the sensual energy which seems to flow from her. She is dressed in a fur jacket and a tight-fitting canary-yellow dress. Sylvester is an Arkansas country boy, the size of a fullback. He wears a new suit and coat, in which he is obviously uncomfortable. Most of the time, he stutters when he speaks.*)

MA RAINEY: Irvin . . . you better tell this man who I am! You better get him straight!

IRVIN: Ma, do you know what time it is? Do you have any idea? We've been waiting . . .

DUSSIE MAE (*To Sylvester*): If you was watching where you was going . . .

SYLVESTER: I was watching . . . What you mean?

IRVIN (*Notices Policeman*): What's going on here? Officer, what's the matter?

MA RAINEY: Tell the man who he's messing with!

POLICEMAN: Do you know this lady?

MA RAINEY: Just tell the man who I am! That's all you gotta do.

POLICEMAN: Lady, will you let me talk, huh?

MA RAINEY: Tell the man who I am!

IRVIN: Wait a minute . . . wait a minute! Let me handle it. Ma, will you let me handle it?

MA RAINEY: Tell him who he's messing with!

IRVIN: Okay! Okay! Give me a chance! Officer, this is one of our recording artists . . . Ma Rainey.

MA RAINEY: Madame Rainey! Get it straight! Madame Rainey! Talking about taking me to jail!

IRVIN: Look, Ma . . . give me a chance, okay? Here . . . sit down. I'll take care of it. Officer, what's the problem?

DUSSIE MAE (*To Sylvester*): It's all your fault.

SYLVESTER: I ain't done nothing . . . Ask Ma.

POLICEMAN: Well . . . when I walked up on the incident . . .

DUSSIE MAE: Sylvester wrecked Ma's car.

SYLVESTER: I d-d-did not! The m-m-man ran into me!

POLICEMAN (*To Irvin*): Look, buddy . . . if you want it in a nutshell, we got her charged with assault and battery.

MA RAINEY: Assault and what for what!

DUSSIE MAE: See . . . we was trying to get a cab . . . and so Ma . . .

MA RAINEY: Wait a minute! I'll tell you if you wanna know what happened. (*Points to Sylvester*) Now, that's Sylvester. That's my nephew. He was driving my car . . .

POLICEMAN: Lady, we don't know whose car he was driving.

MA RAINEY: That's my car!

DUSSIE MAE AND SYLVESTER: That's Ma's car!

MA RAINEY: What you mean you don't know whose car it is? I bought and paid for that car.

POLICEMAN: That's what you say, lady . . . We still gotta check. *(To Irvin)* They hit a car on Market Street. The guy said the kid ran a stoplight.

SYLVESTER: What you mean? The man c-c-come around the comer and hit m-m-me!

POLICEMAN: While I was calling a paddy wagon to haul them to the station, they try to hop into a parked cab. The cabbie said he was waiting on a fare . . .

MA RAINEY: The man was just sitting there. Wasn't waiting for nobody. I don't know why he wanna tell that lie.

POLICEMAN: Look, lady . . . will you let me tell the story?

MA RAINEY: Go ahead and tell it then. But tell it right!

POLICEMAN: Like I say . . . she tries to get in this cab. The cabbie's waiting on a fare. She starts creating a disturbance. The cabbie gets out to try and explain the situation to her . . . and she knocks him down.

DUSSIE MAE: She ain't hit him! He just fell!

SYLVESTER: He just s-s-s-slipped!

POLICEMAN: He claims she knocked him down. We got her charged with assault and battery.

MA RAINEY: If that don't beat all to hell. I ain't touched the man! The man was trying to reach around me to keep his car door closed. I opened the door and it hit him and he fell down. I ain't touched the man!

IRVIN: Okay. Okay . . . I got it straight now, Ma. You didn't touch him. All right? Officer, can I see you for a minute?

DUSSIE MAE: Ma was just trying to open the door.

SYLVESTER: He j-j-just got in t-t-the way!

MA RAINEY: Said he wasn't gonna haul no colored folks . . . if you want to know the truth of it.

IRVIN: Okay, Ma . . . I got it straight now. Officer?

(Irvin pulls the Policeman off to the side.)

MA RAINEY *(Noticing Toledo)*: Toledo, Cutler and everybody here?

TOLEDO: Yeah, they down in the band room. What happened to your car?

STURDYVANT (*Entering*): Irv, what's the problem? What's going on? Officer . . .

IRVIN: Mel, let me take care of it. I can handle it.

STURDYVANT: What's happening? What the hell's going on?

IRVIN: Let me handle it, Mel, huh?

(*Sturdyvant crosses over to Ma Rainey.*)

STURDYVANT: What's going on, Ma? What'd you do?

MA RAINEY: Sturdyvant, get on away from me! That's the last thing I need . . . to go through some of your shit!

IRVIN: Mel, I'll take care of it. I'll explain it all to you. Let me handle it, huh?

(*Sturdyvant reluctantly returns to the control booth.*)

POLICEMAN: Look, buddy, like I say . . . we got her charged with assault and battery . . . and the kid with threatening the cabbie.

SYLVESTER: I ain't done n-n-nothing!

MA RAINEY: You leave the boy out of it. He ain't done nothing. What's he supposed to have done?

POLICEMAN: He threatened the cabbie, lady! You just can't go around threatening people.

SYLVESTER: I ain't done nothing to him! He's the one talking about he g-g-gonna get a b-b-baseball bat on me! I just told him what I'd do with it. But I ain't done nothing 'cause he didn't get the b-b-bat!

IRVIN (*Pulling the Policeman aside*): Officer . . . look here . . .

POLICEMAN: We was on our way down to the precinct . . . but I figured I'd do you a favor and bring her by here. I mean, if she's as important as she says she is . . .

IRVIN (*Slides a bill from his pocket*): Look, Officer . . . I'm Madame Rainey's manager . . . It's good to meet you. (*Shakes the Policeman's hand and passes him the bill*) As soon as we're finished with the recording session, I'll personally stop by the precinct house and straighten up this misunderstanding.

POLICEMAN: Well . . . I guess that's all right. As long as someone is responsible for them. (*Pockets the bill and winks at Irvin*) No need to come down . . . I'll take care of it myself. Of course, we wouldn't want nothing like this to happen again.

IRVIN: Don't worry, Officer . . . I'll take care of everything. Thanks for your help.

(*Irvin escorts the Policeman to the door and returns. He crosses over to Ma Rainey.*)

Here, Ma . . . let me take your coat. (*To Sylvester*) I don't believe I know you.

MA RAINEY: That's my nephew, Sylvester.

IRVIN: I'm very pleased to meet you. Here . . . you can give me your coat.

MA RAINEY: That there is Dussie Mae.

IRVIN: Hello . . . (*Dussie Mae hands Irvin her coat*) Listen, Ma, just sit there and relax. The boys are in the band room rehearsing. You just sit and relax a minute.

MA RAINEY: I ain't for no sitting. I ain't never heard of such. Talking about taking me to jail. Irvin, call down there and see about my car.

IRVIN: Okay, Ma . . . I'll take care of it. You just relax.

(*Irvin exits with the coats.*)

MA RAINEY: Why you all keep it so cold in here? Sturdyvant try and pinch every penny he can. You all wanna make some records, you better put some heat on in here or give me back my coat.

IRVIN (*Entering*): We got the heat turned up, Ma. It's warming up. It'll be warm in a minute.

DUSSIE MAE (*Whispering to Ma Rainey*): Where's the bathroom?

MA RAINEY: It's in the back. Down the hall next to Sturdyvant's office. Come on, I'll show you where it is. Irvin, call down there and see about my car. I want my car fixed today.

IRVIN: I'll take care of everything, Ma. (*Notices Toledo*) Say . . . uh . . . uh . . .

TOLEDO: Toledo.

IRVIN: Yeah . . . Toledo. I got the sandwiches, you can take down to the rest of the boys. We'll be ready to go in a minute. Give you boys a chance to eat and then we'll be ready to go.

(*Irvin and Toledo exit. The lights go down in the studio and come up in the band room.*)

LEVEE: Slow Drag, you ever been to New Orleans?

SLOW DRAG: What's in New Orleans that I want?

LEVEE: How you call yourself a musician and ain't never been to New Orleans.

SLOW DRAG: You ever been to Fat Back, Arkansas? (*Pause*) All right, then. Ain't never been nothing in New Orleans that I couldn't get in Fat Back.

LEVEE: That's why you backwards. You just an old country boy talking about Fat Back, Arkansas, and New Orleans in the same breath.

CUTLER: I been to New Orleans. What about it?

LEVEE: You ever been to Lula White's?

CUTLER: Lula White's? I ain't never heard of it.

LEVEE: Man, they got some gals in there just won't wait! I seen a man get killed in there once. Got drunk and grabbed one

of the gals wrong . . . I don't know what the matter of it
was. But he grabbed her and she stuck a knife in him all
the way up to the hilt. He ain't even fell. He just stood
there and choked on his own blood. I was just asking Slow
Drag 'cause I was gonna take him to Lula White's when
we get down to New Orleans and show him a good time.
Introduce him to one of them gals I know down there.

CUTLER: Slow Drag don't need you to find him no pussy. He
can take care of his own self. Fact is . . . you better watch
your gal when Slow Drag's around. They don't call him
Slow Drag for nothing. (Laughs) Tell him how you got
your name, Slow Drag.

SLOW DRAG: I ain't thinking about Levee.

CUTLER: Slow Drag break a woman's back when he dance.
They had this contest one time in this little town called
Bolingbroke about a hundred miles outside of Macon. We
was playing for this dance and they was giving twenty dollars to the best slow draggers. Slow Drag looked over the
competition, got down off the bandstand, grabbed hold of
one of them gals, and stuck to her like a fly to jelly. Like
wood to glue. Man had that gal whooping and hollering so
. . . everybody stopped to watch. This fellow come in . . .
this gal's fellow . . . and pulled a knife a foot long on Slow
Drag. 'Member that, Slow Drag?

SLOW DRAG: Boy that mama was hot! The front of her dress
was wet as a dishrag!

LEVEE: So what happened? What the man do?

CUTLER: Slow Drag ain't missed a stroke. The gal, she just
look at her man with that sweet dizzy look in her eye. She
ain't about to stop! Folks was clearing out, ducking and
hiding under tables, figuring there's gonna be a fight. Slow
Drag just looked over the gal's shoulder at the man and
said, "Mister, if you'd quit hollering and wait a minute . . .
you'll see I'm doing you a favor. I'm helping this gal win
ten dollars so she can buy you a gold watch." The man just

stood there and looked at him, all the while stroking that knife. Told Slow Drag, say, "All right, then, nigger. You just better make damn sure you win." That's when folks started calling him Slow Drag. The women got to hanging around him so bad after that, them fellows in that town ran us out of there.

(Toledo enters, carrying a small cardboard box with the sandwiches.)

LEVEE: Yeah . . . well, them gals in Lula White's will put a harness on his ass.

TOLEDO: Ma's up there. Some kind of commotion with the police.

CUTLER: Police? What the police up there for?

TOLEDO: I couldn't get it straight. Something about her car. They gone now . . . she's all right. Mr. Irvin sent some sandwiches.

(Levee springs across the room.)

LEVEE: Yeah, all right. What we got here? *(Takes two sandwiches out of the box)*

TOLEDO: What you doing grabbing two? There ain't but five in there . . . How you figure you get two?

LEVEE: 'Cause I grabbed them first. There's enough for everybody . . . What you talking about? It ain't like I'm taking food out of nobody's mouth.

CUTLER: That's all right. He can have mine too. I don't want none.

(Levee starts toward the box to get another sandwich.)

TOLEDO: Nigger, you better get out of here. Slow Drag, you want this?

43

SLOW DRAG: Naw, you can have it.

TOLEDO: With Levee around, you don't have to worry about no leftovers. I can see that.

LEVEE: What's the matter with you? Ain't you eating two sandwiches? Then why you wanna talk about me? Talking about there won't be no leftovers with Levee around. Look at your own self before you look at me.

TOLEDO: That's what you is. That's what we all is. A leftover from history. You see now, I'll show you.

LEVEE: Aw, shit . . . I done got the nigger started now.

TOLEDO: Now, I'm gonna show you how this goes . . . where you just a leftover from history. Everybody come from different places in Africa, right? Come from different tribes and things. Soonawhile they began to make one big stew. You had the carrots, the peas, and potatoes and whatnot over here. And over there you had the meat, the nuts, the okra, corn . . . and then you mix it up and let it cook right through to get the flavors flowing together . . . then you got one thing. You got a stew.

Now you take and eat the stew. You take and make your history with that stew. All right. Now it's over. Your history's over and you done ate the stew. But you look around and you see some carrots over here, some potatoes over there. That stew's still there. You done made your history and it's still there. You can't eat it all. So what you got? You got some leftovers. That's what it is. You got leftovers and you can't do nothing with it. You already making you another history . . . cooking you another meal, and you don't need them leftovers no more. What to do?

See, we's the leftovers. The colored man is the leftovers. Now, what's the colored man gonna do with himself? That's what we waiting to find out. But first we gotta know we the leftovers. Now, who knows that? You find me a nigger that knows that and I'll turn any whichaway you want me to. I'll bend over for you. You ain't gonna find that. And that's what the problem is. The problem ain't with the white man. The white man knows you just a leftover. 'Cause he the one who done the eating and he know what he done ate. But we don't know that we been took and made history out of. Done went and filled the white man's belly and now he's full and tired and wants you to get out the way and let him be by himself. Now, I know what I'm talking about. And if you wanna find out, you just ask Mr. Irvin what he had for supper yesterday. And if he's an honest white man . . . which is asking for a whole heap of a lot . . . he'll tell you he done ate your black ass and if you please I'm full up with you . . . so go on and get off the plate and let me eat something else.

SLOW DRAG: What that mean? What's eating got to do with how the white man treat you? He don't treat you no different according to what he ate.

TOLEDO: I ain't said it had nothing to do with how he treat you.

CUTLER: The man's trying to tell you something, fool!

SLOW DRAG: What he trying to tell me? Ain't you here. Why you say he was trying to tell *me* something? Wasn't he trying to tell you too?

LEVEE: He was trying all right. He was trying a whole heap. I'll say that for him. But trying ain't worth a damn. I got lost right there trying to figure out who puts nuts in their stew.

SLOW DRAG: I knowed that before. My grandpappy used to put nuts in his stew. He and my grandmama both. That ain't nothing new.

TOLEDO: They put nuts in their stew all over Africa. But the stew they eat, and the stew your grandpappy made, and all the stew that you and me eat, and the stew Mr. Irvin eats . . . ain't in no way the same stew. That's the way that go. I'm through with it. That's the last you know me to ever try and explain something to you.

CUTLER (*After a pause*): Well, time's getting along . . . Come on, let's finish rehearsing.

LEVEE (*Stretching out on a bench*): I don't feel like rehearsing. I ain't nothing but a leftover. You go and rehearse with Toledo . . . He's gonna teach you how to make a stew.

SLOW DRAG: Cutler, what you gonna do? I don't want to be around here all day.

LEVEE: I know my part. You all go on and rehearse your part. You all need some rehearsal.

CUTLER: Come on, Levee, get up off your ass and rehearse the songs.

LEVEE: I already know them songs . . . What I wanna rehearse them for?

SLOW DRAG: You in the band, ain't you? You supposed to rehearse when the band rehearse.

TOLEDO: Levee think he the king of the barnyard. He thinks he's the only rooster know how to crow.

LEVEE: All right! All right! Come on, I'm gonna show you I know them songs. Come on, let's rehearse. I bet you the first one mess be Toledo. Come on . . . I wanna see if he know how to crow.

CUTLER: "Ma Rainey's Black Bottom," Levee's version. Let's do it.

(*They begin to rehearse. The lights go down in the band room and up in the studio. Ma Rainey sits and takes off her shoes, rubs her feet. Dussie Mae wanders about looking at the studio. Sylvester is over by the piano.*)

MA RAINEY (*Singing to herself*):
> Oh, Lord, these dogs of mine
> They sure do worry me all the time
> The reason why I don't know
> Lord, I beg to be excused
> I can't wear me no sharp-toed shoes.
> I went for a walk
> I stopped to talk
> Oh, how my corns did bark.

DUSSIE MAE: It feels kinda spooky in here. I ain't never been in no recording studio before. Where's the band at?

MA RAINEY: They off somewhere rehearsing. I don't know where Irvin went to. All this hurry up and he goes off back there with Sturdyvant. I know he better come on 'cause Ma ain't gonna be waiting. Come here . . . let me see that dress.

(Dussie Mae crosses over. Ma Rainey tugs at the dress around the waist, appraising the fit.)

That dress looks nice. I'm gonna take you tomorrow and get you some more things before I take you down to Memphis. They got clothes up here you can't get in Memphis. I want you to look nice for me. If you gonna travel with the show you got to look nice.

DUSSIE MAE: I need me some more shoes. These hurt my feet.

MA RAINEY: You get you some shoes that fit your feet. Don't you be messing around with no shoes that pinch your feet. Ma know something about bad feet. Hand me my slippers out my bag over yonder.

(Dussie Mae brings the slippers.)

DUSSIE MAE: I just want to get a pair of them yellow ones. About a half-size bigger.

MA RAINEY: We'll get you whatever you need. Sylvester, too . . . I'm gonna get him some more clothes. Sylvester, tuck your clothes in. Straighten them up and look nice. Look like a gentleman.

DUSSIE MAE: Look at Sylvester with that hat on.

MA RAINEY: Sylvester, take your hat off inside. Act like your mama taught you something. I know she taught you better than that.

(Sylvester bangs on the piano.)

Come on over here and leave that piano alone.

SYLVESTER: I ain't d-d-doing nothing to the p-p-piano. I'm just l-l-looking at it.

MA RAINEY: Well. Come on over here and sit down. As soon as Mr. Irvin comes back, I'll have him take you down and introduce you to the band.

(Sylvester comes over.)

He's gonna take you down there and introduce you in a minute . . . have Cutler show you how your part go. And when you get your money, you gonna send some of it home to your mama. Let her know you doing all right. Make her feel good to know you doing all right in the world.

(Dussie Mae wanders about the studio and opens the door leading to the band room. The strains of Levee's version of "Ma Rainey's Black Bottom" can be heard. Irvin enters.)

IRVIN: Ma, I called down to the garage and checked on your car. It's just a scratch. They'll have it ready for you this afternoon. They're gonna send it over with one of their fellows.

MA RAINEY: They better have my car fixed right too. I ain't going for that. Brand-new car . . . they better fix it like new.

IRVIN: It was just a scratch on the fender, Ma . . . They'll take care of it . . . don't worry . . . they'll have it like new.

MA RAINEY: Irvin, what is that I hear? What is that the band's rehearsing? I know they ain't rehearsing Levee's "Black Bottom." I know I ain't hearing that?

IRVIN: Ma, listen . . . that's what I wanted to talk to you about. Levee's version of that song . . . it's got a nice arrangement . . . a nice horn intro . . . It really picks it up . . .

MA RAINEY: I ain't studying Levee nothing. I know what he done to that song and I don't like to sing it that way. I'm doing it the old way. That's why I brought my nephew to do the voice intro.

IRVIN: Ma, that's what the people want now. They want something they can dance to. Times are changing. Levee's arrangement gives the people what they want. It gets them excited . . . makes them forget about their troubles.

MA RAINEY: I don't care what you say, Irvin. Levee ain't messing up my song. If he got what the people want, let him take it somewhere else. I'm singing Ma Rainey's song. I ain't singing Levee's song. Now that's all there is to it. Carry my nephew on down there and introduce him to the band. I promised my sister I'd look out for him and he's gonna do the voice intro on the song my way.

IRVIN: Ma, we just figured that . . .

MA RAINEY: Who's this "we"? What you mean "we"? I ain't studying Levee nothing. Come talking this "we" stuff. Who's "we"?

IRVIN: Me and Sturdyvant. We decided that it would—

MA RAINEY: You decided, huh? I'm just a bump on the log. I'm gonna go which ever way the river drift. Is that it? You and Sturdyvant decided.

IRVIN: Ma, it was just that we thought it would be better.

MA RAINEY: I ain't got good sense. I don't know nothing about music. I don't know what's a good song and what ain't. You know more about my fans than I do.

IRVIN: It's not that, Ma. It would just be easier to do. It's more what the people want.

MA RAINEY: I'm gonna tell you something, Irvin . . . and you go on up there and tell Sturdyvant. What you all say don't count with me. You understand? Ma listens to her heart. Ma listens to the voice inside her. That's what counts with Ma. Now, you carry my nephew on down there . . . tell Cutler he's gonna do the voice intro on that "Black Bottom" song and that Levee ain't messing up my song with none of his music shit. Now, if that don't set right with you and Sturdyvant . . . then I can carry my black bottom on back down South to my tour, 'cause I don't like it up here no ways.

IRVIN: Okay, Ma . . . I don't care. I just thought . . .

MA RAINEY: Damn what you thought! What you look like telling me how to sing my song? This Levee and Sturdyvant nonsense . . . I ain't going for it! Sylvester, go on down there and introduce yourself. I'm through playing with Irvin.

SYLVESTER: Which way you go? Where they at?

MA RAINEY: Here . . . I'll carry you down there myself.

DUSSIE MAE: Can I go? I wanna see the band.

MA RAINEY: You stay your behind up here. Ain't no cause in you being down there. Come on, Sylvester.

IRVIN: Okay, Ma. Have it your way. We'll be ready to go in fifteen minutes.

MA RAINEY: We'll be ready to go when Madame says we're ready. That's the way it goes around here.

(Ma Rainey and Sylvester exit. The lights go down in the studio and up in the band room. Ma Rainey enters with Sylvester.)

Cutler, this here is my nephew Sylvester. He's gonna do that voice intro on the "Black Bottom" song using the old version.

LEVEE: What you talking about? Mr. Irvin say he's using my version. What you talking about?

MA RAINEY: Levee, I ain't studying you or Mr. Irvin. Cutler, get him straightened out on how to do his part. I ain't thinking about Levee. These folks done messed with the wrong person this day. Sylvester, Cutler gonna teach you your part. You go ahead and get it straight. Don't worry about what nobody else say.

(Ma Rainey exits.)

CUTLER: Well, come on in, boy. I'm Cutler. You got Slow Drag
. . . Levee . . . and that's Toledo over there. Sylvester,
huh?

SYLVESTER: Sylvester Brown.

LEVEE: I done wrote a version of that song what picks it up
and sets it down in the people's lap! Now she come talking
this! You don't need that old circus bullshit! I know what
I'm talking about. You gonna mess up the song, Cutler,
and you know it.

CUTLER: I ain't gonna mess up nothing. Ma say—

LEVEE: I don't care what Ma say! I'm talking about what the
intro gonna do to the song. The peoples in the North ain't
gonna buy all that tent-show nonsense. They wanna hear
some music!

CUTLER: Nigger, I done told you time and again . . . you just in
the band. You plays the piece . . . whatever they want! Ma
says what to play! Not you! You ain't here to be doing no
creating. Your job is to play whatever Ma says!

LEVEE: I might not play nothing! I might quit!

CUTLER: Nigger, don't nobody care if you quit. Whose heart
you gonna break?

TOLEDO: Levee ain't gonna quit. He got to make some money
to keep him in shoe polish.

LEVEE: I done told you all . . . you all don't know me. You don't
know what I'll do.

CUTLER: I don't think nobody too much give a damn! Sylvester, here's the way your part go. The band plays the
intro . . . I'll tell you where to come in. The band plays the
intro and then you say, "All right, boys, you done seen the
rest . . . Now I'm gonna show you the best. Ma Rainey's
gonna show you her black bottom." You got that?

(Sylvester nods.)

Let me hear you say it one time.

SYLVESTER: "All right, boys, you done s-s-seen the rest n-n-now I'm gonna show you the best. M-m-m-m-m-m-ma Rainey's gonna s-s-show you her black b-b-bottom."

LEVEE: What kind of . . . All right, Cutler! Let me see you fix that! You straighten that out! You hear that shit, Slow Drag? How in the hell the boy gonna do the part and he can't even talk!

SYLVESTER: W-w-w-who's you to tell me what to do, nigger! This ain't your band! Ma tell me to d-d-d-do it and I'm gonna do it. You can go to hell, n-n-n-nigger!

LEVEE: B-b-b-boy, ain't nobody studying you. You go on and fix that one, Cutler. You fix that one and I'll . . . I'll shine your shoes for you. You go on and fix that one!

TOLEDO: You say you Ma's nephew, huh?

SYLVESTER: Yeah. So w-w-what that mean?

TOLEDO: Oh, I ain't meant nothing . . . I was just asking.

SLOW DRAG: Well, come on and let's rehearse so the boy can get it right.

LEVEE: I ain't rehearsing nothing! You just wait till I get my band. I'm gonna record that song and show you how it supposed to go!

CUTLER: We can do it without Levee. Let him sit on over there. Sylvester, you remember your part?

SYLVESTER: I remember it pretty g-g-g-good.

CUTLER: Well, come on, let's do it, then.

(*The band begins to play. Levee sits and pouts. Sturdyvant enters the band room.*)

STURDYVANT: Good . . . you boys are rehearsing, I see.

LEVEE (*Jumping up*): Yessir! We rehearsing. We know them songs real good.

STURDYVANT: Good! Say, Levee, did you finish that song?

LEVEE: Yessir, Mr. Sturdyvant. I got it right here. I wrote that other part just like you say. It go like:

You can shake it, you can break it
You can dance at any hall
You can slide across the floor
You'll never have to stall
My jelly, my roll,
Sweet Mama, don't you let it fall.

Then I put that part in there for the people to dance, like you say, for them to forget about their troubles.
STURDYVANT: Good! Good! I'll just take this. I wanna see you about your songs as soon as I get the chance.
LEVEE: Yessir! As soon as you get the chance, Mr. Sturdyvant.

(Sturdyvant exits.)

CUTLER: You hear, Levee? You hear this nigger? "Yessuh, we's rehearsing, boss."
SLOW DRAG: I heard him. Seen him too. Shuffling them feet.
TOLEDO: Aw, Levee can't help it none. He's like all of us. Spooked up with the white men.
LEVEE: I'm spooked up with him, all right. You let one of them crackers fix on me wrong. I'll show you how spooked up I am with him.
TOLEDO: That's the trouble of it. You wouldn't know if he was fixed on you wrong or not. You so spooked up by him you ain't had the time to study him.
LEVEE: I studies the white man. I got him studied good. The first time one fixes on me wrong, I'm gonna let him know just how much I studied. Come telling me I'm spooked up with the white man. You let one of them mess with me, I'll show you how spooked up I am.
CUTLER: You talking out your hat. The man come in here, call you a boy, tell you to get up off your ass and rehearse, and you ain't had nothing to say to him except, "Yessir!"

LEVEE: I can say "yessir" to whoever I please. What you got to do with it? I know how to handle white folks. I been handling them for thirty-two years, and now you gonna tell me how to do it. Just 'cause I say "yessir" don't mean I'm spooked up with him. I know what I'm doing. Let me handle him my way.

CUTLER: Well, go on and handle it, then.

LEVEE: Toledo, you always messing with somebody! Always agitating somebody with that old philosophy bullshit you be talking. You stay out of my way about what I do and say. I'm my own person. Just let me alone.

TOLEDO: You right, Levee. I apologize. It ain't none of my business that you spooked up by the white man.

LEVEE: All right! See! That's the shit I'm talking about. You all back up and leave Levee alone.

SLOW DRAG: Aw, Levee, we was all just having fun. Toledo ain't said nothing about you he ain't said about me. You just taking it all wrong.

TOLEDO: I ain't meant nothing by it, Levee. (*Pause*) Cutler, you ready to rehearse?

LEVEE: Levee got to be Levee! And he don't need nobody messing with him about the white man—'cause you don't know nothing about me. You don't know Levee. You don't know nothing about what kind of blood I got! What kind of heart I got beating here! (*Pounds his chest*) I was eight years old when I watched a gang of white mens come into my daddy's house and have to do with my mama any way they wanted. (*Pause*)

We was living in Jefferson County, about eighty miles outside of Natchez. My daddy's name was Memphis . . . Memphis Lee Green . . . had him near fifty acres of good farming land. I'm talking about good land! Grow anything you want! He done gone off of shares and bought this land from Mr. Hallie's widow woman after he done passed on. Folks called him an uppity nigger 'cause he done saved and borrowed to where he could buy this land and be independent. *(Pause)*

It was coming on planting time and my daddy went into Natchez to get him some seed and fertilizer. Called me, say, "Levee, you the man of the house now. Take care of your mama while I'm gone." I wasn't but a little boy, eight years old. *(Pause)*

My mama was frying up some chicken when them mens come in that house. Must have been eight or nine of them. She standing there frying that chicken and them mens come and took hold of her just like you take hold of a mule and make him do what you want. *(Pause)*

There was my mama with a gang of white mens. She tried to fight them off, but I could see where it wasn't gonna do her any good. I didn't know what they were doing to her . . . but I figured whatever it was they may as well do to me too. My daddy had a knife that he kept around there for hunting and working and whatnot. I knew where he kept it and I went and got it.

I'm gonna show you how spooked up I was by the white man. I tried my damndest to cut one of them's throat! I hit him on the shoulder with it. He reached back and grabbed hold of that knife and whacked me across the chest with it. *(Raises his shirt to show a long ugly scar)* That's what made them stop. They was scared I was gonna bleed to death. My mama wrapped a sheet around me and carried me two miles down to the Furlow place and they drove me up to Doc Albans. He was waiting on a calf to be born, and say he ain't had time to see me. They carried me up to Miss Etta, the midwife, and she fixed me up.

My daddy came back and acted like he done accepted the facts of what happened. But he got the names of them mens from mama. He found out who they was and then we announced we was moving out of that county. Said good-bye to everybody . . . all the neighbors. My daddy

went and smiled in the face of one of them crackers who
had been with my mama. Smiled in his face and sold him
our land. We moved over with relations in Caldwell. He
got us settled in and then he took off one day. I ain't never
seen him since. He sneaked back, hiding up in the woods,
laying to get them eight or nine men. (*Pause*)

He got four of them before they got him. They
tracked him down in the woods. Caught up with him and
hung him and set him afire. (*Pause*)

My daddy wasn't spooked up by the white man.
Nosir! And that taught me how to handle them. I seen my
daddy go up and grin in this cracker's face . . . smile in his
face and sell him his land. All the while he's planning how
he's gonna get him and what he's gonna do to him. That
taught me how to handle them. So you all just back up
and leave Levee alone about the white man. I can smile
and say "yessir" to whoever I please. I got time coming to
me. You all just leave Levee alone about the white man.

(*There is a long pause. Slow Drag begins playing on the bass.*)

SLOW DRAG (*Singing*):
    If I had my way
    If I had my way
    If I had my way
    I would tear this old building down.

ACT TWO

The lights come up in the studio. The musicians are setting up their instruments. Ma Rainey walks about shoeless, singing softly to herself. Levee stands near Dussie Mae, who hikes up her dress and crosses her leg. Cutler speaks to Irvin off to the side.

CUTLER: Mr. Irvin, I don't know what you gonna do. I ain't got nothing to do with it, but the boy can't do the part. He stutters. He can't get it right. He stutters right through it every time.

IRVIN: Christ! Okay. We'll . . . Shit! We'll just do it like we planned. We'll do Levee's version. I'll handle it, Cutler. Come on, let's go. I'll think of something.

(He exits to the control booth.)

MA RAINEY *(Calling Cutler over)*: Levee's got his eyes in the wrong place. You better school him, Cutler.

CUTLER: Come on, Levee . . . let's get ready to play! Get your mind on your work!

IRVIN (*Over speaker*): Okay, boys, we're gonna do "Moonshine Blues" first. "Moonshine Blues," Ma.

MA RAINEY: I ain't doing no "Moonshine" nothing. I'm doing the "Black Bottom" first. Come on, Sylvester. (*To Irvin*) Where's Sylvester's mike? You need a mike for Sylvester. Irvin . . . get him a mike.

IRVIN: Uh . . . Ma, the boys say he can't do it. We'll have to do Levee's version.

MA RAINEY: What you mean he can't do it? Who say he can't do it? What boys say he can't do it?

IRVIN: The band, Ma . . . the boys in the band.

MA RAINEY: What band? The band work for me! I say what goes! Cutler, what's he talking about? Levee, this some of your shit?

IRVIN: He stutters, Ma. They say he stutters.

MA RAINEY: I don't care if he do. I promised the boy he could do the part . . . and he's gonna do it! That's all there is to it. He don't stutter all the time. Get a microphone down here for him.

IRVIN: Ma, we don't have time. We can't . . .

MA RAINEY: If you wanna make a record, you gonna find time. I ain't playing with you, Irvin. I can walk out of here and go back to my tour. I got plenty fans. I don't need to go through all of this. Just go and get the boy a microphone.

(*Irvin and Sturdyvant consult in the booth, Irvin exits.*)

STURDYVANT: All right, Ma . . . we'll get him a microphone. But if he messes up . . . He's only getting one chance . . . The cost . . .

MA RAINEY: Damn the cost. You always talking about the cost. I make more money for this outfit than anybody else you got put together. If he messes up he'll just do it till he gets it right. Levee, I know you had something to do with this. You better watch yourself.

LEVEE: It was Cutler!

SYLVESTER: It was you! You the only one m-m-mad about it.

LEVEE: The boy stutter. He can't do the part. Everybody see that. I don't know why you want the boy to do the part no ways.

MA RAINEY: Well, can or can't . . . he's gonna do it! You ain't got nothing to do with it!

LEVEE: I don't care what you do! He can sing the whole god-damned song for all I care!

MA RAINEY: Well, all right. Thank you.

(Irvin enters with a microphone and hooks it up. He exits to the control booth.)

Come on, Sylvester. You just stand here and hold your hands like I told you. Just remember the words and say them . . . That's all there is to it. Don't worry about messing up. If you mess up, we'll do it again. Now, let me hear you say it. Play for him, Cutler.

CUTLER: One . . . two . . . You know what to do.

(The band begins to play and Sylvester curls his fingers and clasps his hands together in front of his chest, pulling in opposite directions as he says his lines.)

SYLVESTER: All right, boys, you d-d-d-done s-s-s-seen the best . . .

(Levee stops playing.)

Now I'm g-g-g-gonna show you the rest . . . Ma R-r-rainey's gonna show you her b-b-b-black b-b-b-bottom.

(The rest of the band stops playing.)

MA RAINEY: That's all right. That's real good. You take your time, you'll get it right.

STURDYVANT (*Over speaker*): Listen, Ma . . . now, when you come in, don't wait so long to come in. Don't take so long on the intro, huh?

MA RAINEY: Sturdyvant, don't you go trying to tell me how to sing. You just take care of that up there and let me take care of this down here. Where's my Coke?

IRVIN: Okay, Ma. We're all set up to go up here. "Ma Rainey's Black Bottom," boys.

MA RAINEY: Where's my Coke? I need a Coke. You ain't got no Coke down here? Where's my Coke?

IRVIN: What's the matter, Ma? What's . . .

MA RAINEY: Where's my Coke? I need a Coca-Cola.

IRVIN: Uh . . . Ma, look, I forgot the Coke, huh? Let's do it without it, huh? Just this one song. What say, boys?

MA RAINEY: Damn what the band say! You know I don't sing nothing without my Coca-Cola!

STURDYVANT: We don't have any, Ma. There's no Coca-Cola here. We're all set up and we'll just go ahead and . . .

MA RAINEY: You supposed to have Coca-Cola. Irvin knew that. I ain't singing nothing without my Coca-Cola!

(*She walks away from the mike, singing to herself. Sturdyvant enters from the control booth.*)

STURDYVANT: Now, just a minute here, Ma. You come in an hour late . . . we're way behind schedule as it is . . . the band is set up and ready to go . . . I'm burning my lights . . . I've turned up the heat . . . We're ready to make a record and what? You decide you want a Coca-Cola?

MA RAINEY: Sturdyvant, get out of my face.

(*Irvin enters.*)

Irvin . . . I told you keep him away from me.

IRVIN: Mel, I'll handle it.

STURDYVANT: I'm tired of her nonsense, Irv. I'm not gonna put up with this!

IRVIN: Let me handle it, Mel. I know how to handle her. (*To Ma Rainey*) Look, Ma . . . I'll call down to the deli and get you a Coke. But let's get started, huh? Sylvester's standing there ready to go . . . the band's set up . . . let's do this one song, huh?

MA RAINEY: If you too cheap to buy me a Coke, I'll buy my own. Slow Drag! Sylvester, go with Slow Drag and get me a Coca-Cola.

(*Slow Drag comes over.*)

Slow Drag, walk down to that store on the corner and get me three bottles of Coca-Cola. Get out my face, Irvin. You all just wait until I get my Coke. It ain't gonna kill you.

IRVIN: Okay, Ma. Get your Coke, for Chrissakes! Get your Coke!

(*Irvin and Sturdyvant exit into the hallway, followed by Slow Drag and Sylvester. Toledo, Cutler and Levee head for the band room.*)

MA RAINEY: Cutler, come here a minute. I want to talk to you.

(*Cutler crosses over somewhat reluctantly.*)

What's all this about "the boys in the band say"? I tells you what to do. I says what the matter is with the band. I say who can and can't do what.

CUTLER: We just say 'cause the boy stutter . . .

MA RAINEY: I know he stutters. Don't you think I know he stutters. This is what's gonna help him.

CUTLER: Well, how can he do the part if he stutters? You want him to stutter through it? We just thought it be easier to go on and let Levee do it like we planned.

MA RAINEY: I don't care if he stutters or not! He's doing the part and I don't wanna hear any more of this shit about what the band says. And I want you to find somebody to replace Levee when we get to Memphis. Levee ain't nothing but trouble.

CUTLER: Levee's all right. He plays good music when he puts his mind to it. He knows how to write music too.

MA RAINEY: I don't care what he know. He ain't nothing but bad news. Find somebody else. I know it was his idea about who to say who can do what.

(Dussie Mae wanders over to where they are sitting.)

Dussie Mae, go sit your behind down somewhere and quit flaunting yourself around.

DUSSIE MAE: I ain't doing nothing.

MA RAINEY: Well, just go on somewhere and stay out of the way.

CUTLER: I been meaning to ask you, Ma . . . about these songs. This "Moonshine Blues" . . . that's one of them songs Bessie Smith sang, I believes.

MA RAINEY: Bessie what? Ain't nobody thinking about Bessie. I taught Bessie. She ain't doing nothing but imitating me. What I care about Bessie? I don't care if she sell a million records. She got her people and I got mine. I don't care what nobody else do. Ma was the *first* and don't you forget it!

CUTLER: Ain't nobody said nothing about that. I just said that's the same song she sang.

MA RAINEY: I been doing this a long time. Ever since I was a little girl. I don't care what nobody else do. That's what gets me so mad with Irvin. White folks try to be put out with you all the time. Too cheap to buy me a Coca-Cola.

I lets them know it, though. Ma don't stand for no shit. Wanna take my voice and trap it in them fancy boxes with all them buttons and dials . . . and then too cheap to buy me a Coca-Cola. And it don't cost but a nickel a bottle.

CUTLER: I knows what you mean about that.

MA RAINEY: They don't care nothing about me. All they want is my voice. Well, I done learned that, and they gonna treat me like I want to be treated no matter how much it hurt them. They back there now calling me all kinds of names . . . calling me everything but a child of God. But they can't do nothing else. They ain't got what they wanted yet. As soon as they get my voice down on them recording machines, then it's just like if I'd be some whore and they roll over and put their pants on. Ain't got no use for me then. I know what I'm talking about. You watch. Irvin right there with the rest of them. He don't care nothing about me either. He's been my manager for six years, always talking about sticking together, and the only time he had me in his house was to sing for some of his friends.

CUTLER: I know how they do.

MA RAINEY: If you colored and can make them some money, then you all right with them. Otherwise, you just a dog in the alley. I done made this company more money from my records than all the other recording artists they got put together. And they wanna balk about how much this session is costing them.

CUTLER: I don't see where it's costing them all what they say.

MA RAINEY: It ain't! I don't pay that kind of talk no mind.

(*The lights go down on the studio and come up on the band room. Toledo sits reading a newspaper. Levee sings and hums his song.*)

LEVEE (*Singing*):
    You can shake it, you can break it
    You can dance at any hall

You can slide across the floor
You'll never have to stall
My jelly, my roll,
Sweet Mama, don't you let it fall.

Wait till Sturdyvant hear me play that! I'm talking about some real music, Toledo! I'm talking about *real* music!

(The door opens and Dussie Mae enters.)

Hey, mama! Come on in.

DUSSIE MAE: Oh, hi! I just wanted to see what it looks like down here.

LEVEE: Well, come on in . . . I don't bite.

DUSSIE MAE: I didn't know you could really write music. I thought you was just jiving me at the club last night.

LEVEE: Naw, baby . . . I knows how to write music. I done give Mr. Sturdyvant some of my songs and he says he's gonna let me record them. Ask Toledo. I'm gonna have my own band! Toledo, ain't I give Mr. Sturdyvant some of my songs I wrote?

TOLEDO: Don't get Toledo mixed up in nothing. *(Exits)*

DUSSIE MAE: You gonna get your own band sure enough?

LEVEE: That's right! Levee Green and his Footstompers.

DUSSIE MAE: That's real nice.

LEVEE: That's what I was trying to tell you last night. A man what's gonna get his own band need to have a woman like you.

DUSSIE MAE: A woman like me wants somebody to bring it and put it in my hand. I don't need nobody wanna get something for nothing and leave me standing in my door.

LEVEE: That ain't Levee's style, sugar. I got more style than that. I knows how to treat a woman. Buy her presents and things . . . treat her like she wants to be treated.

DUSSIE MAE: That's what they all say . . . till it come time to be buying the presents.

LEVEE: When we get down to Memphis, I'm gonna show you what I'm talking about. I'm gonna take you out and show you a good time. Show you Levee knows how to treat a woman.

DUSSIE MAE: When you getting your own band?

LEVEE (*Moves closer to slip his arm around her*): Soon as Mr. Sturdyvant say. I done got my fellows already picked out. Getting me some good fellows know how to play real sweet music.

DUSSIE MAE (*Moves away*): Go on now, I don't go for all that pawing and stuff. When you get your own band, maybe we can see about this stuff you talking.

LEVEE (*Moving toward her*): I just wanna show you I know what the women like. They don't call me Sweet Lemonade for nothing.

(*Levee takes her in his arms and attempts to kiss her.*)

DUSSIE MAE: Stop it now. Somebody's gonna come in here.

LEVEE: Naw they ain't. Look here, sugar . . . what I wanna know is . . . can I introduce my red rooster to your brown hen?

DUSSIE MAE: You get your band, then we'll see if that rooster know how to crow.

(*He grinds up against her and feels her buttocks.*)

LEVEE: Now I know why my grandpappy sat on the back porch with his straight razor when Grandma hung out the wash.

DUSSIE MAE: Nigger, you crazy!

LEVEE: I bet you sound like the midnight train from Alabama when it crosses the Mason-Dixon line.

DUSSIE MAE: How's you get so crazy?

LEVEE: It's women like you . . . drives me that way.

(He moves to kiss her as the lights go down in the band room and up in the studio. Ma Rainey sits with Cutler and Toledo.)

MA RAINEY: It sure done got quiet in here. I never could stand no silence. I always got to have some music going on in my head somewhere. It keeps things balanced. Music will do that. It fills things up. The more music you got in the world, the fuller it is.

CUTLER: I can agree with that. I got to have my music too.

MA RAINEY: White folks don't understand about the blues. They hear it come out, but they don't know how it got there. They don't understand that's life's way of talking. You don't sing to feel better. You sing 'cause that's a way of understanding life.

CUTLER: That's right. You get that understanding and you done got a grip on life to where you can hold your head up and go on to see what else life got to offer.

MA RAINEY: The blues help you get out of bed in the morning. You get up knowing you ain't alone. There's something else in the world. Something's been added by that song. This be an empty world without the blues. I take that emptiness and try to fill it up with something.

TOLEDO: You fill it up with something the people can't be without, Ma. That's why they call you the Mother of the Blues. You fill up that emptiness in a way ain't nobody ever thought of doing before. And now they can't be without it.

MA RAINEY: I ain't started the blues way of singing. The blues always been here.

CUTLER: In the church sometimes you find that way of singing. They got blues in the church.

MA RAINEY: They say I started it . . . but I didn't. I just helped it out. Filled up that empty space a little bit. That's all. But if they wanna call me the Mother of the Blues, that's all right with me. It don't hurt none.

(Slow Drag and Sylvester enter with Cokes.)

It sure took you long enough. That store ain't but on the corner.

SLOW DRAG: That one was closed. We had to find another one.

MA RAINEY: Sylvester, go and find Mr. Irvin and tell him we ready to go.

(Sylvester exits. The lights in the band room come up while the lights in the studio dim. Levee and Dussie Mae are kissing. Slow Drag enters. They break their embrace. Dussie Mae straightens up her clothes.)

SLOW DRAG: Cold out. I just wanted to warm up with a little sip. *(Goes to his locker, takes out his bottle and drinks)* Ma got her Coke, Levee. We about ready to start.

(Slow Drag exits. Levee attempts to kiss Dussie Mae again.)

DUSSIE MAE: No . . . Come on! I got to go. You gonna get me in trouble.

(She pulls away and exits up the stairs. Levee watches after her.)

LEVEE: Good God! Happy birthday to the lady with the cakes!

(The lights go down in the band room and come up in the studio. Ma Rainey drinks her Coke. Levee enters from the band room. The musicians take their places. Sylvester stands by his mike. Irvin and Sturdyvant look on from the control booth.)

IRVIN: We're all set up here, Ma. We're all set to go. You ready down there?

MA RAINEY: Sylvester, you just remember your part and say it. That's all there is to it. (*To Irvin*) Yeah, we ready.

IRVIN: Okay, boys. "Ma Rainey's Black Bottom." Take one.

CUTLER: One . . . two . . . You know what to do.

(*The band plays.*)

SYLVESTER: All right boys, you d-d-d-done s-s-seen the rest . . .

IRVIN: Hold it!

(*The band stops. Sturdyvant changes the recording disk and nods to Irvin.*)

Okay. Take two.

CUTLER: One . . . two . . . You know what to do.

(*The band plays.*)

SYLVESTER: All right, boys, you done seen the rest . . . now I'm gonna show you the best. Ma Rainey's g-g-g-gonna s-s-show you her b-b-black bottom.

IRVIN: Hold it! Hold it!

(*The band stops. Sturdyvant changes the recording disk.*)

Okay. Take three. Ma, let's do it without the intro, huh? No voice intro . . . you just come in singing.

MA RAINEY: Irvin, I done told you . . . the boy's gonna do the part. He don't stutter all the time. Just give him a chance. Sylvester, hold your hands like I told you and just relax. Just relax and concentrate.

IRVIN: All right. Take three.

CUTLER: One . . . two . . . You know what to do.

(*The band plays.*)

SYLVESTER: All right, boys, you done seen the rest . . . now, I'm gonna show you the best. Ma Rainey's gonna show you her black bottom.

MA RAINEY (*Singing*):
> Way down south in Alabamy
> I got a friend they call Dancing Sammy
> Who's crazy about all the latest dances
> Black bottom stomping, two babies prancing
>
> The other night at a swell affair
> As soon as the boys found out that I was there
> They said, come on, Ma, let's go to the cabaret.
> When I got there, you ought to hear them say,
>
> I want to see the dance you call the black bottom
> I want to learn that dance
> I want to see the dance you call your big black bottom
> It'll put you in a trance.
>
> All the boys in the neighborhood
> They say your black bottom is really good
> Come on and show me your black bottom
> I want to learn that dance
>
> I want to see the dance you call the black bottom
> I want to learn that dance
> Come on and show the dance you call your big black
>   bottom
> It puts you in a trance.
>
> Early last morning about the break of day
> Grandpa told my grandma, I heard him say,
> Get up and show your old man your black bottom
> I want to learn that dance

(*Instrumental break.*)

I done showed you all my black bottom
You ought to learn that dance.

IRVIN: Okay, that's good, Ma. That sounded great! Good job,
boys!

MA RAINEY (*To Sylvester*): See! I told you. I knew you could do
it. You just have to put your mind to it. Didn't he do good,
Cutler? Sound real good. I told him he could do it.

CUTLER: He sure did. He did better than I thought he was
gonna do.

IRVIN (*Entering to remove Sylvester's mike*): Okay, boys . . . Ma . . .
let's do "Moonshine Blues" next, huh? "Moonshine Blues,"
boys.

STURDYVANT (*Over speaker*): Irv! Something's wrong down
there. We don't have it right.

IRVIN: What? What's the matter, Mel . . .

STURDYVANT: We don't have it right. Something happened.
We don't have the goddamn song recorded!

IRVIN: What's the matter? Mel, what happened? You sure you
don't have nothing?

STURDYVANT: Check that mike, huh, Irv. It's the kid's mike.
Something's wrong with the mike. We've got everything
all screwed up here.

IRVIN: Christ almighty! Ma, we got to do it again. We don't
have it. We didn't record the song.

MA RAINEY: What you mean you didn't record it? What was
you and Sturdyvant doing up there?

IRVIN (*Following the mike wire*): Here . . . Levee must have
kicked the plug out.

LEVEE: I ain't done nothing. I ain't kicked nothing!

SLOW DRAG: If Levee had his mind on what he's doing . . .

MA RAINEY: Levee, if it ain't one thing, it's another. You better
straighten yourself up!

LEVEE: Hell . . . it ain't my fault. I ain't done nothing!

STURDYVANT: What's the matter with that mike, Irv? What's the problem?

IRVIN: It's the cord, Mel. The cord's all chewed up. We need another cord.

MA RAINEY: This is the most disorganized . . . Irvin, I'm going home! Come on. Come on, Dussie.

(Ma Rainey walks past Sturdyvant as he enters from the control booth. She exits offstage to get her coat.)

STURDYVANT *(To Irvin)*: Where's she going?

IRVIN: She said she's going home.

STURDYVANT: Irvin, you get her! If she walks out of here . . .

(Ma Rainey enters carrying her and Dussie Mae's coats.)

MA RAINEY: Come on, Sylvester.

IRVIN *(Helping her with her coat)*: Ma . . . Ma . . . listen. Fifteen minutes! All I ask is fifteen minutes!

MA RAINEY: Come on, Sylvester, get your coat.

STURDYVANT: Ma, if you walk out of this studio . . .

IRVIN: Fifteen minutes, Ma!

STURDYVANT: You'll be through . . . washed up! If you walk out on me . . .

IRVIN: Mel, for Chrissakes, shut up and let me handle it! *(Goes after Ma Rainey, who has started for the door)* Ma, listen. These records are gonna be hits! They're gonna sell like crazy! Hell, even Sylvester will be a star. Fifteen minutes. That's all I'm asking! Fifteen minutes.

MA RAINEY *(Crosses to a chair and sits with her coat on)*: Fifteen minutes! You hear me, Irvin? Fifteen minutes . . . and then I'm gonna take my black bottom on back down to Georgia. Fifteen minutes. Then Madame Rainey is leaving!

IRVIN (*Kisses her*): All right, Ma . . . fifteen minutes. I promise. (*To the band*) You boys go ahead and take a break. Fifteen minutes and we'll be ready to go.

CUTLER: Slow Drag, you got any of that bourbon left?

SLOW DRAG: Yeah, there's some down there.

CUTLER: I could use a little nip.

(*Cutler and Slow Drag exit to the band room, followed by Levee and Toledo. The lights go down in the studio and up in the band room.*)

SLOW DRAG: Don't make me no difference if she leave or not. I was kinda hoping she would leave.

CUTLER: I'm like Mr. Irvin . . . After all this time we done put in here, it's best to go ahead and get something out of it.

TOLEDO: Ma gonna do what she wanna do, that's for sure. If I was Mr. Irvin, I'd best go on and get them cords and things hooked up right. And I wouldn't take no longer than fifteen minutes doing it.

CUTLER: If Levee had his mind on his work, we wouldn't be in this fix. We'd be up there finishing up. Now we got to go back and see if that boy get that part right. Ain't no telling if he ever get that right again in his life.

LEVEE: Hey, Levee ain't done nothing!

SLOW DRAG: Levee up there got one eye on the gal and the other on his trumpet.

CUTLER: Nigger, don't you know that's Ma's gal?

LEVEE: I don't care whose gal it is. I ain't done nothing to her. I just talk to her like I talk to anybody else.

CUTLER: Well, that being Ma's gal, and that being that boy's gal, is one and two different things. The boy is liable to kill you . . . but you ass gonna be out there scraping the concrete looking for a job if you messing with Ma's gal.

LEVEE: How am I messing with her? I ain't done nothing to the gal. I just asked her her name. Now, if you telling me I can't do that, then Ma will just have to go to hell.

CUTLER: All I can do is warn you.

SLOW DRAG: Let him hang himself, Cutler. Let him string his neck out.

LEVEE: I ain't done nothing to the gal! You all talk like I done went and done something to her. Leave me go with my business.

CUTLER: I'm through with it. Try and talk to a fool . . .

TOLEDO: Some mens got it worse than others . . . this foolishness I'm talking about. Some mens is excited to be fools. That excitement is something else. I know about it. I done experienced it. It makes you feel good to be a fool. But it don't last long. It's over in a minute. Then you got to tend with the consequences. You got to tend with what comes after. That's when you wish you had learned something about it.

LEVEE: That's the best sense you made all day. Talking about being a fool. That's the only sensible thing you said today. Admitting you was a fool.

TOLEDO: I admits it, all right. Ain't nothing wrong with it. I done been a little bit of everything.

LEVEE: Now you're talking. You's as big a fool as they make.

TOLEDO: Gonna be a bit more things before I'm finished with it. Gonna be foolish again. But I ain't never been the same fool twice. I might be a different kind of fool, but I ain't gonna be the same fool twice. That's where we parts ways.

SLOW DRAG: Toledo, you done been a fool about a woman?

TOLEDO: Sure. Sure I have. Same as everybody.

SLOW DRAG: Hell, I ain't never seen you mess with no woman. I thought them books was your woman.

TOLEDO: Sure I messed with them. Done messed with a whole heap of them. And gonna mess with some more. But I ain't gonna be no fool about them. What you think? I done come in the world full-grown, with my head in a book? I done been young. Married. Got kids. I done been around and I done loved women to where you shake in your shoes just at the sight of them. Feel it all up and down your spine.

SLOW DRAG: I didn't know you was married.

TOLEDO: Sure. Legally. I been married legally. Got the papers
and all. I done been through life. Made my marks. Followed
some signs on the road. Ignored some others. I done been
all through it. I touched and been touched by it. But I ain't
never been the same fool twice. That's what I can say.

LEVEE: But you been a fool. That's what counts. Talking about
I'm a fool for asking the gal her name and here you is one
yourself.

TOLEDO: Now, I married a woman. A good woman. To this
day I can't say she wasn't a good woman. I can't say nothing bad about her. I married that woman with all the good
graces and intentions of being hooked up and bound to
her for the rest of my life. I was looking for her to put me
in my grave. But, you see . . . it ain't all the time what you
intentions and wishes are. She went out and joined the
church. All right. There ain't nothing wrong with that. A
good Christian woman going to church and wanna do
right by her God. There ain't nothing wrong with that.
But she got up there, got to seeing them good Christian
mens and wondering why I ain't like that. Soon she figure
she got a heathen on her hands. She figured she couldn't
live like that. The church was more important than I was.
So she left. Packed up one day and moved out. To this day
I ain't never said another word to her. Come home one day
and my house was empty! And I sat down and figured out
that I was a fool not to see that she needed something that
I wasn't giving her. Else she wouldn't have been up there at
the church in the first place. I ain't blaming her. I just said
it wasn't gonna happen to me again. So, yeah, Toledo been
a fool about a woman. That's part of making life.

CUTLER: Well, yeah, I been a fool too. Everybody done been a
fool once or twice. But, you see, Toledo, what you call a
fool and what I call a fool is two different things. I can't see
where you was being a fool for that. You ain't done nothing

foolish. You can't help what happened, and I wouldn't call you a fool for it. A fool is responsible for what happens to him. A fool cause it to happen. Like Levee . . . if he keeps messing with Ma's gal and his feet be out there scraping the ground. That's a fool.

LEVEE: Ain't nothing gonna happen to Levee. Levee ain't gonna let nothing happen to him. Now, I'm gonna say it again. I asked the gal her name. That's all I done. And if that's being a fool, then you looking at the biggest fool in the world . . . 'cause I sure as hell asked her.

SLOW DRAG: You just better not let Ma see you ask her. That's what the man's trying to tell you.

LEVEE: I don't need nobody to tell me nothing.

CUTLER: Well, Toledo, all I gots to say is that from the looks of it . . . from your story . . . I don't think life did you fair.

TOLEDO: Oh, life is fair. It's just in the taking what it gives you.

LEVEE: Life ain't shit. You can put it in a paper bag and carry it around with you. It ain't got no balls. Now, death . . . death got some style! Death will kick your ass and make you wish you never been born! That's how bad death is! But you can rule over life. Life ain't nothing.

TOLEDO: Cutler, how's your brother doing?

CUTLER: Who, Nevada? Oh, he's doing all right. Staying in St. Louis. Got a bunch of kids, last I heard.

TOLEDO: Me and him was all right with each other. Done a lot of farming together down in Plattsville.

CUTLER: Yeah, I know you all was tight. He in St. Louis now. Running an elevator, last I hear about it.

SLOW DRAG: That's better than stepping in muleshit.

TOLEDO: Oh, I don't know now. I liked farming. Get out there in the sun . . . smell that dirt. Be out there by yourself . . . nice and peaceful. Yeah, farming was all right by me. Sometimes I think I'd like to get me a little old place . . . but I done got too old to be following behind one of them balky mules now.

LEVEE: Nigger talking about life is fair. And ain't got a pot to piss in.

TOLEDO: See, now, I'm gonna tell you something. A nigger gonna be dissatisfied no matter what. Give a nigger some bread and butter . . . and he'll cry 'cause he ain't got no jelly. Give him some jelly, and he'll cry 'cause he ain't got no knife to put it on with. If there's one thing I done learned in this life, it's that you can't satisfy a nigger no matter what you do. A nigger's gonna make his own dissatisfaction.

LEVEE: Niggers got a right to be dissatisfied. Is you gonna be satisfied with a bone somebody done throwed you when you see them eating the whole hog?

TOLEDO: You lucky they let you be an entertainer. They ain't got to accept your way of entertaining. You lucky and don't even know it. You's entertaining and the rest of the people is hauling wood. That's the only kind of job for the colored man.

SLOW DRAG: Ain't nothing wrong with hauling wood. I done hauled plenty wood. My daddy used to haul wood. Ain't nothing wrong with that. That's honest work.

LEVEE: That ain't what I'm talking about. I ain't talking about hauling no wood. I'm talking about being satisfied with a bone somebody done throwed you. That's what's the matter with you all. You satisfied sitting in one place. You got to move on down the road from where you sitting . . . and all the time you got to keep an eye out for that devil who's looking to buy up souls. And hope you get lucky and find him!

CUTLER: I done told you about that blasphemy. Talking about selling your soul to the devil.

TOLEDO: We done the same thing, Cutler. There ain't no difference. We done sold Africa for the price of tomatoes. We done sold ourselves to the white man in order to be like him. Look at the way you dressed . . . That ain't African. That's the white man. We trying to be just like

him. We done sold who we are in order to become someone else. We's imitation white men.

CUTLER: What else we gonna be, living over here?

LEVEE: I'm Levee. Just me. I ain't no imitation nothing!

SLOW DRAG: You can't change who you are by how you dress.
That's what I got to say.

TOLEDO: It ain't all how you dress. It's how you act, how you
see the world. It's how you follow life.

LEVEE: It don't matter what you talking about. I ain't no imitation white man. And I don't want to be no white man.
As soon as I get my band together and make them records
like Mr. Sturdyvant done told me I can make, I'm gonna
be like Ma and tell the white man just what he can do. Ma
tell Mr. Irvin she gonna leave . . . and Mr. Irvin get down
on his knees and beg her to stay! That's the way I'm gonna
be! Make the white man respect me!

CUTLER: The white man don't care nothing about Ma. The
colored folks made Ma a star. White folks don't care nothing about who she is . . . what kind of music she make.

SLOW DRAG: That's the truth about that. You let her go down
to one of them white-folks hotels and see how big she is.

CUTLER: Hell, she ain't got to do that. She can't even get a cab
up here in the North. I'm gonna tell you something.
Reverend Gates . . . you know Reverend Gates? Slow Drag
know who I'm talking about. Reverend Gates . . . now I'm
gonna show you how this go where the white man don't
care a thing about who you is. Reverend Gates was coming from Tallahassee to Atlanta, going to see his sister,
who was sick at that time with the consumption. The
train come up through Thomasville, then past Moultrie,
and stopped in this little town called Sigsbee . . .

LEVEE: You can stop telling that right there! That train don't
stop in Sigsbee. I know what train you talking about. That
train got four stops before it reach Macon to go on to

Atlanta. One in Thomasville, one in Moultrie, one in Cordele . . . and it stop in Centerville.

CUTLER: Nigger, I know what I'm talking about. You gonna tell me where the train stop?

LEVEE: Hell, yeah, if you talking about it stop in Sigsbee. I'm gonna tell you the truth.

CUTLER: I'm talking about *this* train! I don't know what train you been riding. I'm talking about *this* train!

LEVEE: Ain't but one train. Ain't but one train come out of Tallahassee heading north to Atlanta, and it don't stop at Sigsbee. Tell him, Toledo . . . that train don't stop at Sigsbee. The only train that stops at Sigsbee is the Yazoo Delta, and you have to transfer at Moultrie to get it!

CUTLER: Well, hell, maybe that what he done! I don't know. I'm just telling you the man got off the train at Sigsbee . . .

LEVEE: All right . . . you telling it. Tell it your way. Just make up anything.

SLOW DRAG: Levee, leave the man alone and let him finish.

CUTLER: I ain't paying Levee no never mind.

LEVEE: Go on and tell it your way.

CUTLER: Anyway . . . Reverend Gates got off this train in Sigsbee. The train done stopped there and he figured he'd get off and check the schedule to be sure he arrive in time for somebody to pick him up. All right. While he's there checking the schedule, it come upon him that he had to go to the bathroom. Now, they ain't had no colored rest rooms at the station. The only colored rest room is an outhouse they got sitting way back two hundred yards or so from the station. All right. He in the outhouse and the train go off and leave him there. He don't know nothing about this town. Ain't never been there before—in fact, ain't never even heard of it before.

LEVEE: I heard of it! I know just where it's at . . . and he ain't got off no train coming out of Tallahassee in Sigsbee!

CUTLER: The man standing there, trying to figure out what he's gonna do . . . where this train done left him in this strange town. It started getting dark. He see where the sun's getting low in the sky and he's trying to figure out what he's gonna do, when he noticed a couple of white fellows standing across the street from this station. Just standing there, watching him. And then two or three more come up and joined the other ones. He look around, ain't seen no colored folks nowhere. He didn't know what was getting in these here fellows' minds, so he commence to walking. He ain't knowed where he was going. He just walking down the railroad tracks when he hear them call him. "Hey, nigger!" See, just like that. "Hey, nigger!" He kept on walking. They called him some more and he just keep walking. Just going down the tracks. And then he heard a gunshot where somebody done fired a gun in the air. He stopped then, you know.

TOLEDO: You don't even have to tell me no more. I know the facts of it. I done heard the same story a hundred times. It happened to me too. Same thing.

CUTLER: Naw, I'm gonna show you how the white folks don't care nothing about who or what you is. They crowded around him. These gang of mens made a circle around him. Now he's standing there, you understand . . . got his cross around his neck like them preachers wear. Had his little Bible with him what he carry all the time. So they crowd on around him and one of them ask who he is. He told them he was Reverend Gates and that he was going to see his sister who was sick and the train left without him. And they said, "Yeah, nigger . . . but can you dance?" He looked at them and commenced to dancing. One of them reached up and tore his cross off his neck. Said he was committing a heresy by dancing with a cross and Bible. Took his Bible and tore it up and had him dancing till they got tired of watching him.

SLOW DRAG: White folks ain't never had no respect for the colored minister.

CUTLER: That's the only way he got out of there alive . . . was to dance. Ain't even had no respect for a man of God! Wanna make him into a clown. Reverend Gates sat right in my house and told me that story from his own mouth. So . . . the white folks don't care nothing about Ma Rainey. She's just another nigger who they can use to make some money.

LEVEE: What I wants to know is . . . if he's a man of God, then where the hell was God when all of this was going on? Why wasn't God looking out for him? Why didn't God strike down them crackers with some of this lightning you talk about to me?

CUTLER: Levee, you gonna burn in hell.

LEVEE: What I care about burning in hell? You talk like a fool . . . burning in hell. Why didn't God strike some of them crackers down? Tell me that! That's the question! Don't come telling me this burning-in-hell shit! He a man of God . . . why didn't God strike some of them crackers down? I'll tell you why! I'll tell you the truth! It's sitting out there as plain as day! 'Cause he a white man's God. That's why! God ain't never listened to no nigger's prayers. God take a nigger's prayers and throw them in the garbage. God don't pay niggers no mind. In fact . . . God hate niggers! Hate them with all the fury in his heart. Jesus don't love you, nigger! Jesus hate your black ass! Come talking that shit to me. Talking about burning in hell! God can kiss my ass.

(Cutler can stand no more. He jumps up and punches Levee in the mouth. The force of the blow knocks Levee down and Cutler jumps on him.)

CUTLER: You worthless . . . That's my God! That's my God! That's my God! You wanna blaspheme my God!

(Toledo and Slow Drag grab Cutler and try to pull him off Levee.)

80

slow drag: Come on, Cutler . . . let it go! It don't mean nothing!

(Cutler has Levee down on the floor and pounds on him with a fury.)

cutler: Wanna blaspheme my God! You worthless . . . talking about my God!

(Toledo and Slow Drag succeed in pulling Cutler off Levee, who is bleeding at the nose and mouth.)

levee: Naw, let him go! Let him go! *(Pulls out a knife)* That's your God, huh? That's your God, huh? Is that right? Your God, huh? All right. I'm gonna give your God a chance. I'm gonna give your God a chance. I'm gonna give him a chance to save your black ass.

(Levee circles Cutler with the knife. Cutler picks up a chair to protect himself.)

toledo: Come on, Levee . . . put the knife up!
levee: Stay out of this, Toledo!
toledo: That ain't no way to solve nothing.

(Levee alternately swipes at Cutler during the following.)

levee: I'm calling Cutler's God! I'm talking to Cutler's God! You hear me? Cutler's God! I'm calling Cutler's God. Come on and save this nigger! Strike me down before I cut his throat!
slow drag: Watch him, Cutler! Put that knife up, Levee!
levee *(To Cutler):* I'm calling your God! I'm gonna give him a chance to save you! I'm calling your God! We gonna find out whose God he is!
cutler: You gonna burn in hell, nigger!

LEVEE: Cutler's God! Come on and save this nigger! Come on and save him like you did my mama! Save him like you did my mama! I heard her when she called you! I heard her when she said, "Lord, have mercy! Jesus, help me! Please, God, have mercy on me, Lord Jesus, help me!" And did you turn your back? Did you turn your back, motherfucker? Did you turn your back?

(Levee becomes so caught up in his dialogue with God that he forgets about Cutler and begins to stab upward in the air, trying to reach God.)

Come on! Come on and turn your back on me! Turn your back on me! Come on! Where is you? Come on and turn your back on me! Turn your back on me, motherfucker! I'll cut your heart out! Come on, turn your back on me! Come on! What's the matter? Where is you? Come on and turn your back on me! Come on, what you scared of? Turn your back on me! Come on! Coward, motherfucker!

(Levee folds his knife and stands triumphantly.)

Your God ain't shit, Cutler.

(The lights fade to black.)

MA RAINEY *(Singing)*:
     Ah, you hear me talking to you
     I don't bite my tongue
     You wants to be my man
     You got to fetch it with you when you come.

(Lights come up in the studio. The last bars of the last song of the session are dying out.)

IRVIN (*Over speaker*): Good! Wonderful! We have that, boys. Good session. That's great, Ma. We've got ourselves some winners.

TOLEDO: Well, I'm glad that's over.

MA RAINEY: Slow Drag, where you learn to play the bass at? You had it singing! I heard you! Had that bass jumping all over the place.

SLOW DRAG: I was following Toledo. Nigger got them long fingers striding all over the piano. I was trying to keep up with him.

TOLEDO: That's what you supposed to do, ain't it? Play the music. Ain't nothing abstract about it.

MA RAINEY: Cutler, you hear Slow Drag on that bass? He make it do what he want it to do! Spank it just like you spank a baby.

CUTLER: Don't be telling him that. Nigger's head get so big his hat won't fit him.

SLOW DRAG: If Cutler tune that guitar up, we would really have something!

CUTLER: You wouldn't know what a tuned-up guitar sounded like if you heard one.

TOLEDO: Cutler was talking. I heard him moaning. He was all up in it.

MA RAINEY: Levee . . . what is that you doing? Why you playing all them notes? You play ten notes for every one you supposed to play. It don't call for that.

LEVEE: You supposed to improvise on the theme. That's what I was doing.

MA RAINEY: You supposed to play the song the way I sing it. The way everybody else play it. You ain't supposed to go off by yourself and play what you want.

LEVEE: I was playing the song. I was playing it the way I felt it.

MA RAINEY: I couldn't keep up with what was going on. I'm trying to sing the song and you up there messing up my ear. That's what you was doing. Call yourself playing music.

LEVEE: Hey . . . I know what I'm doing. I know what I'm doing, all right. I know how to play music. You all back up and leave me alone about my music.

CUTLER: I done told you . . . it ain't about *your* music. It's about *Ma's* music.

MA RAINEY: That's all right, Cutler. I done told you what to do.

LEVEE: I don't care what you do. You supposed to improvise on the theme. Not play note for note the same thing over and over again.

MA RAINEY: You just better watch yourself. You hear me?

LEVEE: What I care what you or Cutler do? Come telling me to watch myself. What's that supposed to mean?

MA RAINEY: All right . . . you gonna find out what it means.

LEVEE: Go ahead and fire me. I don't care. I'm gonna get my own band anyway.

MA RAINEY: You keep messing with me.

LEVEE: Ain't nobody studying you. You ain't gonna do nothing to me. Ain't nobody gonna do nothing to Levee.

MA RAINEY: All right, nigger . . . you fired!

LEVEE: You think I care about being fired? I don't care nothing about that. You doing me a favor.

MA RAINEY: Cutler, Levee's out! He don't play in my band no more.

LEVEE: I'm fired . . . Good! Best thing that ever happened to me. I don't need this shit!

(Levee exits to the band room. Irvin enters from the control booth.)

MA RAINEY: Cutler, I'll see you back at the hotel.

IRVIN: Okay, boys . . . you can pack up. I'll get your money for you.

CUTLER: That's cash money, Mr. Irvin. I don't want no check.

IRVIN: I'll see what I can do. I can't promise you nothing.

CUTLER: As long as it ain't no check. I ain't got no use for a check.

IRVIN: I'll see what I can do, Cutler.

(Cutler, Toledo and Slow Drag exit to the band room.)

Oh, Ma, listen . . . I talked to Sturdyvant, and he said . . .
Now, I tried to talk him out of it . . . He said the best he
can do is to take your twenty-five dollars of your money
and give it to Sylvester.

MA RAINEY: Take what and do what? If I wanted the boy to
have twenty-five dollars of my money, I'd give it to him.
He supposed to get his own money. He supposed to get
paid like everybody else.

IRVIN: Ma, I talked to him . . . He said . . .

MA RAINEY: Go talk to him again! Tell him if he don't pay
that boy, he'll never make another record of mine again.
Tell him that. You supposed to be my manager. All this
talk about sticking together. Start sticking! Go on up
there and get that boy his money!

IRVIN: Okay, Ma . . . I'll talk to him again. I'll see what I can
do.

MA RAINEY: Ain't no see about it! You bring that boy's money
back here!

*(Irvin exits. The lights dim in the studio and come up in the band
room. The men have their instruments packed and sit waiting for
Irvin to come and pay them. Slow Drag has a pack of cards.)*

SLOW DRAG: Come on, Levee, let me show you a card trick.

LEVEE: I don't want to see no card trick. What you wanna
show me for? Why you wanna bother me with that?

SLOW DRAG: I was just trying to be nice.

LEVEE: I don't need you to be nice to me. What I need you to
be nice to me for? I ain't gonna be nice to you. I ain't even
gonna let you be in my band no more.

SLOW DRAG: Toledo, let me show you a card trick.

CUTLER: I just hope Mr. Irvin don't bring no check down here. What the hell I'm gonna do with a check?

SLOW DRAG: All right now . . . pick a card. Any card . . . go on . . . take any of them. I'm gonna show you something.

TOLEDO (*Taking a card*): I agrees with you, Cutler. I don't want no check either.

CUTLER: It don't make no sense to give a nigger a check.

SLOW DRAG: Okay, now. Remember your card. Remember which one you got. Now . . . put it back in the deck. Anywhere you want. I'm gonna show you something.

(*Toledo puts the card in the deck.*)

You remember your card? All right. Now I'm gonna shuffle the deck. Now . . . I'm gonna show you what card you picked. Don't say nothing now. I'm gonna tell you what card you picked.

CUTLER: Slow Drag, that trick is as old as my mama.

SLOW DRAG: Naw, naw . . . wait a minute! I'm gonna show him his card . . . There it go! The six of diamonds. Ain't that your card? Ain't that it?

TOLEDO: Yeah, that's it . . . the six of diamonds.

SLOW DRAG: Told you! Told you I'd show him what it was!

(*The lights fade in the band room and come up full on the studio. Sturdyvant enters with Irvin.*)

STURDYVANT: Ma, is there something wrong? Is there a problem?

MA RAINEY: Sturdyvant, I want you to pay that boy his money.

STURDYVANT: Sure, Ma. I got it right here. Two hundred for you and twenty-five for the kid, right?

(*Sturdyvant hands the money to Irvin, who hands it to Ma Rainey and Sylvester.*)

Irvin misunderstood me. It was all a mistake. Irv made a mistake.

MA RAINEY: A mistake, huh?

IRVIN: Sure, Ma. I made a mistake. He's paid, right? I straightened it out.

MA RAINEY: The only mistake was when you found out I hadn't signed the release forms. That was the mistake. Come on, Sylvester.

(She starts to exit.)

STURDYVANT: Hey, Ma . . . come on, sign the forms, huh?

IRVIN: Ma . . . come on now.

MA RAINEY: Get your coat, Sylvester. Irvin, where's my car?

IRVIN: It's right out front, Ma. Here . . . I got the keys right here. Come on, sign the forms, huh?

MA RAINEY: Irvin, give me my car keys!

IRVIN: Sure, Ma . . . just sign the forms, huh?

(He gives her the keys, expecting a trade-off.)

MA RAINEY: Send them to my address and I'll get around to them.

IRVIN: Came on, Ma . . . I took care of everything, right? I straightened everything out.

MA RAINEY: Give me the pen, Irvin. *(Signs the forms)* You tell Sturdyvant . . . one more mistake like that and I can make my records someplace else. *(Turns to exit)* Sylvester, straighten up your clothes. Come on, Dussie Mae.

(She exits, followed by Dussie Mae and Sylvester. The lights go down in the studio and come up on the band room.)

CUTLER: I know what's keeping him so long. He up there writing out checks. You watch. I ain't gonna stand for it.

He ain't gonna bring me no check down here. If he do, he's gonna take it right back upstairs and get some cash.

TOLEDO: Don't get yourself all worked up about it. Wait and see. Think positive.

CUTLER: I am thinking positive. He positively gonna give me some cash. Man give me a check last time . . . you remember . . . we went all over Chicago trying to get it cashed. See a nigger with a check, the first thing they think is he done stole it someplace.

LEVEE: I ain't had no trouble cashing mine.

CUTLER: I don't visit no whorehouses.

LEVEE: You don't know about my business. So don't start nothing. I'm tired of you as it is. I ain't but two seconds off your ass no way.

TOLEDO: Don't you all start nothing now.

CUTLER: What the hell I care what you tired of. I wasn't even talking to you. I was talking to this man right here.

(Irvin and Sturdyvant enter.)

IRVIN: Okay boys. Mr. Sturdyvant has your pay.

CUTLER: As long as it's cash money, Mr. Sturdyvant. 'Cause I have too much trouble trying to cash a check.

STURDYVANT: Oh, yes . . . I'm aware of that. Mr. Irvin told me you boys prefer cash, and that's what I have for you. *(Starts handing out the money)* That was a good session you boys put in . . . That's twenty-five for you. Yessir, you boys really know your business and we are going to . . . Twenty-five for you . . . We are going to get you back in here real soon . . . twenty-five . . . and have another session so you can make some more money . . . and twenty-five for you. Okay, thank you, boys. You can get your things together and Mr. Irvin will make sure you find your way out.

IRVIN: I'll be out front when you get your things together, Cutler.

(*Irvin exits. Sturdyvant starts to follow.*)

LEVEE: Mr. Sturdyvant, sir. About them songs I give you?

STURDYVANT: Oh, yes, . . . uh . . . Levee. About them songs you gave me. I've thought about it and I just don't think the people will buy them. They're not the type of songs we're looking for.

LEVEE: Mr. Sturdyvant, sir . . . I done got my band picked out and they's real good fellows. They knows how to play real good. I know if the peoples hear the music, they'll buy it.

STURDYVANT: Well, Levee, I'll be fair with you . . . but they're just not the right songs.

LEVEE: Mr. Sturdyvant, you got to understand about that music. That music is what the people is looking for. They's tired of jug-band music. They wants something that excites them. Something with some fire to it.

STURDYVANT: Okay, Levee. I'll tell you what I'll do. I'll give you five dollars apiece for them. Now that's the best I can do.

LEVEE: I don't want no five dollars, Mr. Sturdyvant. I wants to record them songs, like you say.

STURDYVANT: Well, Levee, like I say . . . they just aren't the kind of songs we're looking for.

LEVEE: Mr. Sturdyvant, you asked me to write them songs. Now, why didn't you tell me that before when I first give them to you? You told me you was gonna let me record them. What's the difference between then and now?

STURDYVANT: Well, look . . . I'll pay you for your trouble . . .

LEVEE: What's the difference, Mr. Sturdyvant? That's what I wanna know.

STURDYVANT: I had my fellows play your songs, and when I heard them, they just didn't sound like the kind of songs I'm looking for right now.

LEVEE: You got to hear *me* play them, Mr. Sturdyvant! You ain't heard *me* play them. That's what's gonna make them sound right.

STURDYVANT: Well, Levee, I don't doubt that really. It's just that . . . well, I don't think they'd sell like Ma's records. But I'll take them off your hands for you.

LEVEE: The people's tired of jug-band music, Mr. Sturdyvant. They wants something that's gonna excite them! They wants something with some fire! I don't know what fellows you had playing them songs . . . but if I could play them! I'd set them down in the people's lap! Now you told me I could record them songs!

STURDYVANT: Well, there's nothing I can do about that. Like I say, it's five dollars apiece. That's what I'll give you. I'm doing you a favor. Now, if you write any more, I'll help you out and take them off your hands. The price is five dollars apiece. Just like now.

(He attempts to hand Levee the money, finally shoves it in Levee's coat pocket and is gone in a flash. Levee follows him to the door and it slams in his face. He takes the money from his pocket, balls it up and throws it on the floor. The other musicians silently gather up their belongings. Toledo walks past Levee and steps on his shoe.)

LEVEE: Hey! Watch it . . . Shit, Toledo! You stepped on my shoe!

TOLEDO: Excuse me there, Levee.

LEVEE: Look at that! Look at that! Nigger, you stepped on my shoe. What you do that for?

TOLEDO: I said I'm sorry.

LEVEE: Nigger gonna step on my goddamn shoe! You done fucked up my shoe! Look at that! Look at what you done to my shoe, nigger! I ain't stepped on your shoe! What you wanna step on my shoe for?

CUTLER: The man said he's sorry.

LEVEE: Sorry! How the hell he gonna be sorry after he gone ruint my shoe? Come talking about sorry! *(Turns his attention back to Toledo)* Nigger, you stepped on my shoe! You know that! (*Snatches his shoe off his foot and holds it up for Toledo to see*) See what you done?

TOLEDO: What you want me to do about it? It's done now. I said excuse me.

LEVEE: Wanna go and fuck up my shoe like that. I ain't done nothing to your shoe. Look at this!

(*Toledo turns and continues to gather up his things. Levee spins him around by his shoulder.*)

Naw . . . naw . . . look what you done! (*Shoves the shoe in Toledo's face*) Look at that! That's my shoe! Look at that! You did it! You did it! You fucked up my shoe! You stepped on my shoe with them raggedy-ass clodhoppers!

TOLEDO: Nigger, ain't nobody studying you and your shoe! I said excuse me. If you can't accept that, then the hell with it. What you want me to do?

(*Levee is in a near rage, breathing hard. He is trying to get a grip on himself, as even he senses, or perhaps only he senses, he is about to lose control. He looks around, uncertain of what to do. Toledo has gone back to packing, as have Cutler and Slow Drag. They purposefully avoid looking at Levee in hopes he'll calm down if he doesn't have an audience. All the weight in the world suddenly falls on Levee and he rushes at Toledo with his knife in his hand.*)

LEVEE: Nigger, you stepped on my shoe!

(*He plunges the knife into Toledo's back up to the hilt. Toledo lets out a sound of surprise and agony. Cutler and Slow Drag freeze. Toledo falls backward with Levee, his hand still on the knife, holding him up. Levee is suddenly faced with the realization of what he has done. He shoves Toledo forward and takes a step back. Toledo slumps to the floor.*)

He . . . he stepped on my shoe. He did. Honest, Cutler, he stepped on my shoe. What he do that for? Toledo, what you do that for? Cutler, help me. He stepped on my shoe, Cutler. (*Turns his attention to Toledo*) Toledo! Toledo, get up. (*Moves to Toledo and tries to pick him up*) It's okay, Toledo. Come on . . . I'll help you. Come on, stand up now. Levee'll help you.

(*Toledo is limp and heavy and awkward. He slumps back to the floor. Levee gets mad at him.*)

Don't look at me like that! Toledo! Nigger, don't look at me like that! I'm warning you, nigger! Close your eyes! Don't you look at me like that! (*Turns to Cutler*) Tell him to close his eyes. Cutler. Tell him don't look at me like that.
CUTLER: Slow Drag, get Mr. Irvin down here.

(*The sound of a trumpet is heard, Levee's trumpet, a muted trumpet struggling for the highest of possibilities and blowing pain and warning.*
    Blackout.)

END OF PLAY

August Wilson

April 27, 1945–October 2, 2005

August Wilson authored *Gem of the Ocean, Joe Turner's Come and Gone, Ma Rainey's Black Bottom, The Piano Lesson, Seven Guitars, Fences, Two Trains Running, Jitney, King Hedley II* and *Radio Golf*. These works explore the heritage and experience of African Americans, decade by decade, over the course of the twentieth century. Mr. Wilson's plays have been produced at regional theaters across the country, on Broadway and throughout the world. In 2003, Mr. Wilson made his professional stage debut in his one-man show *How I Learned What I Learned*.

Mr. Wilson's work garnered many awards, including the Pulitzer Prize for *Fences* (1987) and *The Piano Lesson* (1990); a Tony Award for *Fences*; Great Britain's Olivier Award for *Jitney*; and eight New York Drama Critics Circle awards for *Ma Rainey's Black Bottom, Fences, Joe Turner's Come and Gone, The Piano Lesson, Two Trains Running, Seven Guitars, Jitney* and *Radio Golf*. Additionally, the cast recording of *Ma Rainey's Black Bottom* received a 1985 Grammy Award, and Mr. Wilson received a 1995 Emmy Award nomination for his screenplay adaptation of *The Piano Lesson*. Mr. Wilson's early works include the one-act plays: *The Janitor, Recycle, The Coldest Day of the Year, Malcolm X, The Homecoming* and the musical satire *Black Bart and the Sacred Hills*.

Mr. Wilson received many fellowships and awards, including Rockefeller and Guggenheim fellowships in playwriting, the Whiting Writers Award and the 2003 Heinz Award. He was awarded a 1999 National Humanities Medal by the President of the United States, and received numerous honorary degrees from colleges and universities, as well as the only high school diploma ever issued by the Carnegie Library of Pittsburgh.

He was an alumnus of New Dramatists, a member of the American Academy of Arts and Sciences, a 1995 inductee into the American Academy of Arts and Letters, and on October 16, 2005, Broadway renamed the theater located at 245 West 52nd Street: The August Wilson Theatre. In 2007, he was posthumously inducted into the Theater Hall of Fame.

Mr. Wilson was born and raised in the Hill District of Pittsburgh, and lived in Seattle at the time of his death. He is survived by two daughters, Sakina Ansari and Azula Carmen Wilson, and his wife, costume designer Constanza Romero.